Editing Activities from *The Blair Handbook* with Additional Items

 A Blair Press Book
PRENTICE HALL, ENGLEWOOD CLIFFS, NJ 07632

©1994 by PRENTICE-HALL, Inc.
A Paramount Communications Company
Englewood Cliffs, NJ 07632

10 9 8 7 6 5 4 3 2 1

ISBN 0-13-954173-X
Printed in the United States of America

Contents

Contents (continued)

■ ■ ■

Improving Openings and Conclusions

■ **Activity 24–1**

Following are the opening and closing paragraphs from a draft of a paper about the difficulties that recent college graduates are having finding suitable jobs. Edit each paragraph to make it more direct and engaging and to sharpen its focus. More than one edited version is possible.

As everybody knows, today we live in a very competitive society. Jobs are harder to find than they were ten years ago, especially for young people just entering the work force. The American dream of success seems to have died. For example, my brother graduated from college with a degree in marketing. He had a high average and many good recommendations from his professors. Yet, after two years, he is still looking for a job in his field. Working as an assistant manager in a hardware store, he can barely make his student loan and car payments, let alone afford rent, so he is still living at home with our parents.

In conclusion, I would like to say that I think it is everyone's responsibility to see that recent college graduates have a better chance. In my opinion, colleges should provide better career counseling. and more businesses should provide training opportunities. I think a voluntary program that would let students work off college loans through government-supported jobs is a good idea. Also, students need to do more career-related planning throughout their four years in school.

■ **Activity 24–2** (Editing 1 in Chapter 24 of *The Blair Handbook*)

24a Making openings engaging

Edit the following opening paragraph to make it more engaging. More than one edited version is possible.

Dr. Ravi Batra, an economist at Southern Methodist University, has described a long-term cycle of economic indicators. Those indicators, he believes, forecast a depression in the next few years. The World Futurist Society also predicts a global economic collapse rivaling the Great Depression of the 1930s. Both predictions cite the rash of bank failures in recent years, implying that the first indication of wider economic troubles will be the downfall of financial institutions.

■ **Activity 24–3** (Editing 2 in Chapter 24 of *The Blair Handbook*)

24b Strengthening weak openings

Edit the following opening paragraph to strengthen it. More than one edited version is possible.

Our society today faces many problems. One of these is the problem of high dropout rates among high school students. Several of my friends who dropped out of high school are now happily unemployed or working at dead-end jobs for low wages. In fact, I was almost a dropout myself. I think if administrators could understand the reasons why dropouts leave and why I decided to stay, they might be able to help other students finish school.

Activity 24–4 (Editing 5 in Chapter 24 of *The Blair Handbook*)

24c Making conclusions satisfying

Edit the following conclusion to make it more satisfying. More than one edited version is possible.

Computers have radically altered our society and will undoubtedly continue to do so. But how far will computers take us? Will we like our destination? From the banking and finance industries to recreation and art, every aspect of our lives has been affected by the ramifications of RAM and ROM. Much as the Industrial Revolution and the Agricultural Revolution did in past centuries the Computer Revolution will fundamentally transform our culture in ways we cannot yet imagine. The three distinctive characteristics of computer transactions—speed of computation, ease of replication, and access through networking—are unremarkable in themselves, but when combined they change the very nature of information, the currency of our culture. No longer is knowledge accumulated over the centuries, unalterably fixed on pieces of paper, and painstakingly consulted when needed. Today's information resembles a rushing torrent always changing, impossible to contain or chart, and ready to sweep aside all limits or restrictions.

Activity 24–5 (Editing 6 in Chapter 24 of *The Blair Handbook*)

24d Strengthening weak conclusions

Edit the following conclusion to strengthen it. More than one edited version is possible.

If the fighting ceases, parents can begin to talk to their children about the divorce and why it happened. From such discussions, children may learn that marriage is not something to rush into, which can be a good thing to learn. As they grow older, the emotional scar they will carry is knowing that their parents did not have a happy marriage, but I think that can be a good thing as well as a painful one.

■ ■ ■

Shaping Strong Paragraphs

■ Activity 25-1

Edit the following paragraph to make it unified, well organized, and coherent, by eliminating any extraneous sentences, shifting and combining sentences so the ideas flow more logically, and adding transitional expressions to connect ideas. You may wish to divide this into more than one paragraph. More than one edited version is possible.

The Vietnam Veterans Memorial in Washington, D.C., was dedicated in 1982. It is another example of a work of public art that caused an outcry. Now it is recognized as a moving tribute to the soldiers who died fighting in Vietnam. When the original design was adopted, many veterans' groups were angry and critical. The monument consists of a seamless black marble slab that extends for several hundred yards, carved with the names of those who died, according to their date of death. At either end, the monument is only a few feet high, reflecting the lower number of casualties at the beginning and end of the war. From each end, visitors follow a path downward, and the dark monument gradually increases in height so that at its center it blocks everything from view except the rows of names of the dead. Visitors can locate the names they are looking for by consulting a booklet prepared by the Park Service. Early critics felt that the monument would appear negative and demeaning to those who died in Vietnam and insisted that a more conventional statue depicting heroic soldiers in combat be erected adjacent to the monument. Very few people spend much time looking at this statue. The monument is now perceived as a superior piece of public art. Family members and friends come back many times to touch the names of their loved ones, to leave messages and flowers, and to weep quietly for those who died in a controversial war.

Activity 25-2 (Editing I in Chapter 25 of *The Blair Handbook*)

25a Ensuring that paragraphs are unified

Strengthen the following paragraphs by editing to ensure unity.

A.   College radio stations do not receive lavish gifts, but they are not neglected in the grand sweep of promotions that back college-targeted records. The station I worked at has received everything from posters to gold records to bottles of liquor. Whether the promotions actually get records played is hard to document. The most common gifts are passes to performances and free copies of records.

B.   The idea of planning seems simple enough. Communities are asked to designate areas for specific purposes, such as commercial, residential, or industrial use. The state's new requirement that every city and township formulate a plan may create a shortage of planners. Trying to pinpoint exactly what a planner does is a little more complicated.

Activity 25-3 (Editing 3 in Chapter 25 of *The Blair Handbook*)

25b Ensuring that paragraphs are well organized

Strengthen the following paragraphs by editing to improve organization.

A.   The machine sucks the milk out of the cows with a vacuum. The vacuum pulsates so that the cows' teats won't lose circulation. Eight cows were lined up in the milking parlor, chewing their cuds and waiting to be mechanically milked. The workers put a black rubber tube over each teat on each cow's udder and turned on the milking machine. The milk flows through clear plastic hoses into glass jars and is siphoned from there into a tank.

B.   After the state legislature passed the Interstate Banking Act of 1987, First State Bank approached state regulators with a plan to merge with the Bank of the Ozarks. Interstate banking is new to the banking industry. Legislation passed before the Great Depression barred interstate banking in an effort to reduce the potential of bank failures and focus banks' investments on their own communities. Given that history, a merger plan like First State's should be evaluated for its effects on local communities and on the stability of the newly created bank.

Activity 25-4 (Editing 6 in Chapter 25 in *The Blair Handbook*)

25c Ensuring that paragraphs are coherent

Strengthen the following paragraph by editing to improve coherence. Consider the use of transitional expressions, the order of sentences, and the use of repetition. More than one edited version is possible.

The number of people accepted at the detoxification center is another issue. If they are violent or if they need specialized medical attention, those brought to the center are not allowed to stay. These policies would seem to restrict the center's effectiveness in reaching everyone who needs help. However, the director, Wanda Rasmussen, defends them as necessary to protect the staff and make sure resources are used efficiently. Others may not have a high enough blood alcohol level to warrant detoxification. About half the people brought to the center are turned away and sent to the "drunk tank" at the city jail.

■ **Activity 25-5** (Editing 9 in Chapter 25 of *The Blair Handbook*)

25c Ensuring that paragraphs are coherent

Strengthen the following passage by editing to improve its coherence. More than one edited version is possible.

The zoning board rejected the proposal. The plan was the subject of three evenings of raucous debate. Then the city council took it up on appeal. The disagreement continued there for months. Some members said their first responsibility was to promote economic development in any form. The debate on the council reflected the divisions in the community. Growth should be regulated so that it does not harm existing businesses or the city as a whole, others believed. The project was approved two weeks after the new mayor took office. Amanda Robbins campaigned for mayor by rallying downtown businesspeople, historic preservationists, and neighborhood activists against the mall. Council member Steven McMillan ran on a pro-development, pro-mall platform. Both candidates said they wanted voters to end the deadlock on the proposal. The election was won by McMillan.

Strengthening Sentence Structure

■ Activity 26–1

Edit the following paragraph to strengthen sentence structure. Use coordination and subordination to relate ideas, eliminate any overuse of coordination and subordination, and create parallelism where it is effective. More than one edited version is possible.

Some communities have succeeded in banning pornography completely. They have been able to close down businesses even when there was no chance of the X-rated materials falling into the hands of minors, and the town of Venice in Florida is a good example. A video store owner there kept X-rated videos in a separate locked room. Customers for these videos had to ask at the counter for a special key, and they had to present three forms of identification, and they also had to sign a special consent form, but some conservative members of the community learned about the business, and they were outraged and notified town officials. Police investigated the reports. Two days later the shop closed down. The owner chose not to challenge the town's ordinance against pornography because he wanted to avoid more negative publicity because he owned several other businesses that he did not want to suffer. In Venice, community pressure and quick legal action have made buying, selling, and even to rent pornography impossible.

■ Activity 26–2 (Editing I in Chapter 26 of *The Blair Handbook*)

26a Using coordination to relate equal ideas
26b Using coordination to combine choppy sentences

Edit the following passage, using coordination to relate ideas of equal importance and to combine choppy sentences. More than one edited version is possible.

The workers were instructed to seal the oiled rags in cans. They forgot to do it. At night the rags caught fire. The fire spread rapidly through the storage area. A smoke detector went off. No one noticed. The alarm was relayed to the fire station. Fire fighters raced to the warehouse. Flames already were darting through the windows. Smoke poured through the ceiling. Glass cracked in the heat. It shattered. The fire commander turned in a second alarm. Another company sped toward the scene.

■ Activity 26–3 (Editing 3 in Chapter 26 of *The Blair Handbook*)

26d Avoiding ineffective coordination

Edit the following passage to eliminate ineffective coordination. More than one edited version is possible.

At the start of *The Bridge across Forever,* the narrator is a stunt pilot performing in small towns of the American Midwest, and the narrator and the author seem to have much in common. The author writes about flying, and the narrator takes people for rides in his plane, but he is bored with the routine, but he is convinced that he will find the perfect woman at one of these shows, so he keeps going. Disillusioned at last, he gives up flying to pursue his quest, and he encounters many women, but none of them is the soul mate he is seeking.

Activity 26–4 (Editing 4 in Chapter 26 of *The Blair Handbook*)

26e Using subordination to distinguish main ideas
26f Using subordination to combine choppy sentences

Edit the following passage, using subordination to clarify the relationships between ideas and to eliminate choppiness. More than one edited version is possible.

Ellen Goodman grabs our attention. She does not let it go for an entire article. Her occasional use of wit or irony makes us laugh. Also she makes us aware of problems around us. She offers no solutions. She is not so much trying to change the world single-handed. She is trying to inspire us to set wrongs to right.

Activity 26–5 (Editing 5 in Chapter 26 of *The Blair Handbook*)

26g Avoiding ineffective coordination

Edit the following passage to eliminate ineffective subordination. More than one edited version is possible.

The Doors completes what could be termed a sixties trilogy from Oliver Stone, since it differs greatly from *Platoon* and *Born on the Fourth of July*. Stone served in Vietnam, although that part of his work is grounded in personal experience. Because he did not experience the world of the Doors, Stone portrays it as he imagines it was, which makes his work in this film different from the others, although it is less effective and less compelling.

Activity 26–6 (Editing 8 in Chapter 26 of *The Blair Handbook*)

26h Creating parallel structures

26i Using parallelism for emphasis

Strengthen sentence structures in the following paragraph by using parallelism and elliptical structures. More than one edited version is possible.

The first cut on *Hope Chest* by 10,000 Maniacs uses a reggae sound in th keyboard. It has an insistent bass line and a guitar that sounds like a swarm of mosquitoes. The vocals are so intricately woven that during the bridge, two sets of lyrics are being sung at once. That sound creates the effect of a breakdown. It also creates the impression of the dissolving of structure.

Activity 26–7 (Editing 9 in Chapter 26 of *The Blair Handbook*)

26j Making parallel structures complete

Edit the following paragraph to correct faulty parallelism. More than one edited version is possible.

First it rained then hail was falling, and finally snow came down. As the temperature dropped we moved our bedrolls closer to the fire, hung blankets over the windows, and more logs were added to the blaze. Nothing seemed to help. The thin walls seemed to invite the cold in. The wind whistled through cracks. The windows rattled in the wind. Snow drifted under the door.

■ **Activity 26–8** (Editing 10 in Chapter 26 of *The Blair Handbook*)

Edit the following passage to strengthen sentence structure, using coordination, subordination, parallel structures, and elliptical structures as you think appropriate. Many edited versions are possible.

Whether Hunter S. Thompson's world is reality or imagined, it makes for enjoyable reading. His humor arises from situations that are so frantic or such exaggerations as to be ludicrous. The writing moves from subject to subject, and it mimics the pattern of a drunken or drugged mind. His sentences ramble. His thoughts tumble. His subjects shift like colors in a hallucination. He somehow maintains a sense of reality. Each description and phrase somehow contain a sharp shard of observation. The reader gets the feeling that his scenes could have happened. Many of them are completely farfetched. He stretches our willingness to believe to the limit. This is the key to Thompson's style.

■ ■ ■

Achieving Emphasis and Variety

■ **Activity 27-1**

Edit the following paragraph to provide emphasis and variety throughout. Be sure that sentences vary in length and type and that not all sentences begin with the subject. You may want to make deliberate use of repetition and elliptical construction and change a sentence or two to questions or exclamations. More than one edited version is possible.

I have started to observe students' body language in class only recently. Students in a group discussion, for example, reveal their moods and their reactions to others through various body movements. Students who feel that their opinions are being attacked will often cross their arms or legs. They may turn their bodies slightly from the rest of the group. This helps them feel set apart and protected. Students who are expressing an opinion they are uncertain about will often lightly touch their upper lips or their noses. This is a way of unconsciously hiding their mouths. Students who are bored or having trouble concentrating on the discussion often sit back and rest one hand on their foreheads. Students who are interested and following the discussion closely often lean forward and place one hand under their chins. Eager students are likely to fidget, shy students are likely to keep very still, and unprepared students are likely to tap their hands or feet in a rhythm. I am not sure about my own body language in these situations because I am always too busy observing everybody else. Body language, in fact, is often more interesting to me than the subject of the discussion.

■ Activity 27–2 (Editing 2 in Chapter 27 of *The Blair Handbook*)

27b Editing sentence length

Edit the following passage, varying the length of the sentences to improve emphasis and variety. More than one edited version is possible.

When I heard the mail drop through the slot in the door, my heart leapt. After I practically flew downstairs, I pounced on the mail that lay scattered on the floor. There, finally, was a letter for me from Iowa State University. "Today's the day," I said to myself, "the day that will seal my fate." At last I would have the answer to the all-important question of whether I had been accepted at the school of my choice. I wondered where I would spend the next four years. I wondered if I would be in Ames, Iowa, or home in Deerfield, Illinois. After I took a deep breath and counted to three, I ripped open the envelope.

■ Activity 27–3

27c Varying sentence types

Edit the following passage, varying the types of sentences to improve emphasis and variety. More than one edited version is possible.

Alcohol and alcohol abuse have been a part of our society for many centuries. Alcoholism has long been regarded as a major health problem. It is now the third greatest killer in the United States. Many individuals and organizations view alcoholism as an illness. The minds and bodies of alcoholics are ill. They are unable to control their drinking. They consequently eventually harm not only themselves but also others. Much is being done in this country to help alcoholics. Probably the best-known source is Alcoholics Anonymous. Many individual states are also starting to build centers to help alcoholics. These centers provide support and therapy. They aim to help alcoholics realize that drinking is not the answer to their problems. It is an admirable goal.

Activity 27–4 (Editing 4 in Chapter 27 of *The Blair Handbook*)

27d Varying sentence openings

To improve the emphasis and variety of the following passage, edit it by beginning some of the sentences with an element other than the subject. More than one edited version is possible.

The College Recruiting Network is a good resource for students and one of the best ways to get a job. The network, provided by campus career development centers, is available across the United States. Forty percent of all students make use of the service, according to studies published last year. Seniors find the network helpful most often, particularly when they don't know what they want to do when they graduate. The network was developed and implemented especially with these students in mind. Students have the opportunity to get involved in the interviewing process early on thanks to the network. Many are, consequently, able to find a job even before they graduate.

■ Activity 27–5 (Editing 6 in Chapter 27 of *The Blair Handbook*)

27f Creating elliptical constructions

Edit the following sentences to create elliptical constructions wherever you think they would be effective. Some sentences can be edited in more than one way.

1. In our family, I am the bossy one, Tom is the quiet one, and Cheryl is the friendly one.

2. Whenever we visited our grandparents' farm, we had to weed and prune in the garden until the marigolds were immaculate, the beans were beautiful, and the pea plants were pristine.

3. Our conversation would be on the virtue of hard work; our thoughts would be on the pleasures of a lazy afternoon.

4. Cheryl and I could usually convince Tom that she was too weak for this sort of work and I was too old.

5. By supper time, Tom's eyes were bleary, and his arms were exhausted, but he was happy to have finally finished.

Activity 27–6 (Editing 8 in Chapter 27 of *The Blair Handbook*)

27   Achieving emphasis and variety

Edit the following passage to provide emphasis and variety throughout. Be sure that sentences vary in length and type and that not all sentences begin with the subject. Try to make use of deliberate repetition and elliptical construction. More than one edited version is possible.

Sunday dinner at Grandma's house was about as appealing as a day without recess to me, an energetic nine-year-old. It meant leaving the kids at the playing field at the bottom of the eighth inning. I had to take a bath in the middle of the day and wash behind my ears. The worst thing was that I had to put on my best clothes and try to keep them clean. For me to keep my clothes clean seemed beyond the realm of possibility in those days. My parents would look absolutely delighted as I emerged from the bath every week. I looked, frankly, nothing like myself. My father would exclaim, "She's as clean as a hound's tooth!" Yet I would arrive at Grandma's week after week looking like Raggedy Ann, despite my best efforts. My shirt would inevitably be stained, my stockings would inevitably be split, my shoes would inevitably be scuffed. My mother would look at me in disbelief as I climbed out of the car. She was amazed, no doubt that such a metamorphosis could have occurred in a twenty-minute car ride. My disheveled appearance, to be honest, never seemed to bother Grandma. She always exclaimed, "Don't you look nice!" I don't know to this day whether she was losing her eyesight or just being kind.

■ ■ ■
Adjusting Tone

■ Activity 28–1

Edit the following passage from a literary analysis to maintain an appropriate academic tone. More than one edited version is possible.

It's wild how completely different the three main characters in Tennessee Williams's *Streetcar Named Desire* are from each other. First, you have Blanche. She's this hard-nosed Southern belle who pretends to be all delicate and helpless, but really she's a major control freak who's always ordering everybody around and making a big deal to get her own way. You feel sorry for her sometimes, but she gets on your nerves too. The play begins when Blanche crashes with her baby sister, Stella, and her sister's husband, Stanley. Now, Stella is this sweet, basic sort of person. (How did these two *ever* get to be sisters?) She'd like to tell Blanche where to get off, but she just doesn't have the guts. So Blanche moves in, and then things get sort of hairy. Stanley is this dumb, low-class kind of guy with no manners but lots of macho. He and Blanche just don't hit it off at all: he thinks she's a lying witch, and she thinks he's an animal. At the same time, though, she's very flirty with him, which doesn't help matters. Sweet little Stella, of course, is right in the middle, having to defend Stanley to Blanche and Blanche to Stanley. You just have this foreboding that the situation is going to become volatile.

Activity 28–2 (Editing 2 in Chapter 28 of *The Blair Handbook*)

28c Achieving the right level of formality

Edit the following two paragraphs, adjusting the tone to the appropriate level of formality. The first paragraph is from a paper relating a personal experience; the second is from a formal research paper. More than one edited version of each paragraph is possible.

Personal Experience Essay

Who would find it credible that two adults would have trouble convincing one eight-pound feline that the time had come for his annual physical examination? Upon spotting his cage, the cat exits the room as quickly as he can. Under the bed, over the bed, up the staircase, down the staircase, he rushes with extreme celerity from one room to the next, ever eluding our grasp. When his outrageous behavior ceases, and we have him cornered, I stealthily approach him and apprehend him. I loudly proclaim myself triumphant as I deposit him in his place of confinement and secure the top.

Formal Research Paper

At the Dryden Correctional Center, the guys who run the education department try to prepare the inmates for living on the outside. That way criminals won't (they hope!) turn back to a life of crime. OK. Sounds like a good idea. But how do they do it? Well they make sure that as soon as the criminals get tossed in the slammer they start getting an education. This is so that they will have a better chance of getting jobs when they get out. The way they figure it is if the criminals get jobs, they won't have to turn to crime to make money. The educational programs are completely voluntary. Lots of the inmates take them, though.

Activity 28–3 (Editing 4 in Chapter 28 of *The Blair Handbook*)

28e Maintaining consistency

Edit the following passage from a formal research essay, removing any inappropriate shifts in tone. More than one edited version is possible.

Whenever a newspaper is acquired by a large chain, a number of events typically follow, as the impact is felt in numerous areas. One common occurrence is that reporters who leave or retire are not replaced. As the staff decreases, so, usually, does the local news. With the decrease in local news, discounts in local advertising rates naturally disappear. Often the newspaper starts publishing a Sunday paper. You don't have to be a rocket scientist to know why they add a Sunday paper. Sunday papers are filled with ads, which means the bosses can really rake in the big bucks. Newspapers that do these things are usually rolling in money within a few years. But don't you think they're really selling out?

Activity 28–4 (Editing 6 in Chapter 28 of *The Blair Handbook*)

28   Adjusting tone

Edit the following passage from a formal argumentative essay, making sure to maintain a consistent, appropriate tone. More than one edited version is possible.

You can really see the similarities between Shakespeare's *King Lear* and Jane Smiley's novel *A Thousand Acres*. Smiley makes you think of Shakespeare's play on purpose, and she expects you to be with it enough to catch on. You can see the parallels even in the names she gives to her characters. The three sisters in *A Thousand Acres* are named Ginny, Rose, and Caroline. These names make you think of Lear's daughters, Goneril, Regan, and Cordelia. Get it? (The first letters are the same.) In both the play and the novel, one really important idea is how parents and kids get along. In Smiley's story, Caroline, the youngest daughter, doesn't like her father's plan to retire and divide his huge farm among his three daughters, so he chills her. In *King Lear*, Cordelia, also the youngest, won't compete with her sisters in telling her old dad how crazy about him she is just so she can get the largest part of his kingdom. In both works, the two older sisters tell their dad what he wants to hear, but the youngest stands up to him.

■ ■ ■
Building Vital Sentences

■ Activity 29–1

Edit the following paragraph to create more vital sentences. Substitute specific, concrete nouns and modifiers for more general ones, and replace weak or static verbs with more descriptive ones. Change passive voice verbs to the active voice where appropriate. Supply creative details wherever necessary. More than one edited version is possible.

The party was going on when I got there. Loud music was coming from the big speakers, and lots of people were on the dance floor. They looked hot and seemed unaware of their surroundings as they moved wildly to the music. As I looked around for my two friends who had got me to come, I made the observation that the walls were covered with four different colors of spirals, which made the room seem to go around. I felt a little dizzy and wanted to sit down. I tried to locate a chair, but they all seemed to be taken. Suddenly, a strange-looking person in a weird outfit came up to me. He or she—couldn't tell if it was a man or a woman—said something I couldn't hear and then laughed and was gone. My stomach began to feel funny, my head was hurting, and I was nervous. "There's nothing to worry about," I told myself. "Try to have a good time." I moved through the crowd, looking for a familiar face. A drink was given to me by someone I didn't know, and it spilled all over me. I decided that it was time to go home.

Activity 29-2 (Editing I in Chapter 29 of *The Blair Handbook*)

29a Using concrete, specific nouns and modifiers

Edit the following paragraph by using concrete, specific nouns and modifiers. You may invent and add whatever details you think are necessary. More than one edited version is possible.

Our college library is really good. Not only does it have lots of books, but it also has plenty of periodicals. Many resources are available to help people with any research we might need to do, and the staff is always ready to give guidance. Last year the library finally finished installing the new computer system. Now we can look up an item in the library from any of the several remote computer terminals located around campus. With just a few keystrokes we can determine whether the library owns the item and, if so, whether it is available or currently in circulation.

Activity 29-3 (Editing 3 in Chapter 29 of *The Blair Handbook*)

29b Choosing strong verbs

Edit the following paragraph by using strong verbs. Make any small changes in wording that are needed for smooth reading. More than one edited version is possible.

Bilingual education is becoming more of a hot topic of debate every year. Some educators make the argument that young children have a need for linguistic continuity between their homes and their classrooms. There is, in fact, a good deal of evidence that does support this view. These educators are strong advocates of programs that use a child's primary language for most classroom instruction while having him or her learn English as a second language. Over the years, the child is speaking English for more and more of the classroom day, until finally he or she is able to join a mainstream classroom.

■ Activity 29–4 (Editing 5 in Chapter 29 of *The Blair Handbook*)

29c Selecting active or passive voice

Edit the following paragraph by using the active voice wherever it is effective. Make any small changes in wording that are necessary for smooth reading. More than one edited version is possible.

We are all affected by pesticides. Hundreds of synthetic chemicals have been developed by scientists to destroy the insects and rodents that are called "pests" by farmers and Sunday gardeners. Once these deadly toxins are used, however, they don't just go away. They are maintained in the environment, where our crops and water supply are contaminated and desirable species of birds and fish are killed off. Ironically, pesticides are even known not to work very well in the first place, since usually a pest population that is resistant to the chemicals is created. And within a few years, it's just as large as ever. Pesticides' effect on the environment and on our lives should be questioned. Perhaps even the right to use them at all should be questioned.

■ Activity 29–5

29d Untangling noun clusters

Edit the following paragraph, untangling noun clusters. Make any small changes in wording that are needed for smooth reading. More than one edited version is possible.

Quilts are once again becoming fashionable. Quilting is the newest amateur home decoration needlework craze. People all over America are rushing to create fake antiques and heirlooms-to-be. The best thing about making your own quilt is that you can pick colors and patterns that quilters of bygone days would never have dreamed of. Of course, if you don't have the time and energy to make a quilt, you can buy a quilt made by someone else. Both antique hand-stitched muslin farmhouse quilts and newer machine-made quilts in designer colors are gaining in popularity and in value.

■ **Activity 29–6** (Editing 7 in Chapter 29 of *The Blair Handbook*)

29   Building vital sentences

Edit the following paragraph to create vital sentences. You may invent and add any details you think are necessary. More than one edited version is possible.

Most dog owners don't realize in advance how much time, money, and energy must be spent on a puppy. First, there is housebreaking the puppy and teaching it basic puppy obedience skills: how to accompany its owner while on a leash, how to respond to its name, how to stay near its owner. There are also other things—fetching, standing, and so on. And even when owners have the time for training they probably don't have the necessary expertise. This means enrollment in expensive obedience school classes is required. Puppies have other expenses as well. Veterinarian visits, food and bedding, leashes and playthings, and grooming—a must for any well-bred dog—are all costly. And at least one nice rug or one pair of shoes must be replaced because a bad dog has chewed through them. Still, as any devoted dog owner will tell you, the expense is justified by the rewards: there's nothing like coming home from a hard day and being greeted by someone who loves you unconditionally and absolutely.

■■■
Being Concise and Direct

■ **Activity 30–1**

Edit the following passage to make it more direct and concise by deleting or simplifying wordy constructions, eliminating redundancy, simplifying grammatical constructions, and replacing pretentious or overblown language. More than one edited version is possible.

According to the administration's survey of applicants for parking stickers, one-half, or fifty percent, of the students who were questioned do not believe that parking is a problem on campus. This number is somewhat misleading, however, due to the fact that the majority of the students who answered this way are full-time residents who live on campus. It is not very likely that most residents move their vehicles on a daily basis, and when they do, they most often do so in the evening hours when spaces are maximized and easier to access. On the other hand, commuting students are compelled to do battle every single, solitary day in the never-ending war for a parking space, and they do so in the busy daytime hours between 8:00 A.M. in the morning and 12:00 noon when there are the greatest number of cars that are entering onto the campus. There is absolutely no question that these students without a doubt have the opinion that parking on campus is a problem of crucial importance, as is so clearly evidenced by the administration's survey. In point of fact, more than ninety percent of those who gave the response that parking is a problem are commuters.

Activity 30–2 (Editing 2 in Chapter 30 of *The Blair Handbook*)

30a Eliminating vague generalities

30b Removing idle words

30c Simplifying grammatical structures

30d Eliminating redundancies

Edit the following passage to make it more direct and concise, eliminating vague generalities, idle words, and redundancies and simplifying grammatical constructions. More than one edited version is possible.

Many languages have influenced the development of English. The first instance of important influence came from the north in the form of Viking invaders who spoke a Scandinavian language. It appears that when these Vikings settled down and became farmers and traders who were peaceful, they wanted to be able to communicate with and speak to their Anglo-Saxon neighbors. There were several factors involved. Both groups spoke Germanic languages with similar vocabularies but with systems of grammar and inflection that were somewhat different. Clearly the easiest of the ways to smooth communication was for each group to drop the elements of its language that gave the other group difficulty. This explains why it is the case that modern English lacks the elaborate systems of verb endings and gender that characterize and distinguish other Indo-European languages.

Activity 30–3 (Editing 2 in Chapter 30 of *The Blair Handbook*)

30e Avoiding pretentious language
30f Minimizing euphemism and misdirection

Edit the following passage to make it more direct and concise, eliminating pretentious language, euphemism, or misdirection. More than one edited version is possible.

The photography exhibit scheduled to appear at the Mainfield Gallery has been postponed because of protests by a local community organization, which has voiced a concern about the photographic depiction of minors au naturel. This is a minority view, however. Moderates who might find fault with photographs showing acts of intimacy between consenting adults see no problem with the scheduled exhibit. And of course, those in the community who firmly espouse the sacred freedom of speech guaranteed by our forefathers would support the exhibit no matter how offensive or injurious to the moral fiber of our young people.

Activity 30–4 (Editing 5 in Chapter 30 of *The Blair Handbook*)

30   Being concise and direct

Edit the following passage to make it more direct and concise. More than one edited version is possible.

My great-grandfather emigrated from Poland when he was a young man. Several of his cousins already lived in small Pennsylvania mining towns. When my great-grandfather arrived in America, he joined his cousins and began working in the mines. There were several things he found discouraging. The dirty work, which was also dangerous, was far different from the life of agricultural splendor he had expected to lead, but he refused to let these types of circumstances ruin his happiness. It eventually was the case that he brought two of his brothers over to this country, and together the three of them saved money that was sufficient to buy a good-sized farm. By the age of thirty-four, my great-grandfather had once again started a new life: he moved into his farmhouse, married a local woman, and began raising a family that would eventually be blessed by the arrival of fourteen bundles of joy.

■ ■ ■

Choosing the Right Word

Edit the following passage to improve word choice. Look for problems with denotation and connotation, easily confused words, standard use of prepositions, slang, and jargon. Use a dictionary and a thesaurus, if you wish, to help you find the best word in each case. More than one edited version is possible.

The program provisions troubled adolescents with mentors who act both as roll models and as councilors. These volunteers, most of whom have experienced tempestuous childhoods themselves, can really get into the problems of teens, helping them improve self-esteem and actualize their true potentialities. During biweekly one-on-one meetings, mentors set down with program participants to help with homework, chat about any problems they may be experiencing home- or school-wise, and share impertinent life experiences. Mentors may also take participants to outings on sporting events, cultural institutes, and business settings. In addition, mentors and participants meet twice a month for group sessions under the direction of a program administor. They discuss goals and stumble blocks, participate in conscienceness-raising exercises, and strategize ways to control anger and channel positive energy. The affect has been positive on all involved.

Activity 31–2 (Editing 1 in Chapter 31 of *The Blair Handbook*)

31a Understanding the history of English

31b Using the dictionary and thesaurus

For each of the words below, think of as many synonyms and near synonyms as you can. Try to guess which words on your list came from Old English, which from French, which from Latin or Greek, and which from other languages. Use a dictionary to confirm your guesses. You may want to compare your word list with your classmates'.

house

happy

angry

light

street

walk

Activity 31–3 (Editing 2 in Chapter 31 of *The Blair Handbook*)

31b Using the dictionary and thesaurus

Use a dictionary and a thesaurus to look up any words that seem unfamiliar or that might be misused in the following passage. Edit the passage by substituting more familiar words and correcting any misuses while preserving the intended meaning.

The role of Emma Woodhouse in Jane Austen's novel *Emma* often receives censure for her supercilious behavior. Many readers consider her attitude toward her neighbors to be unconscionable: she avoids calling on them whenever possible and suffers their visits with scarcely concealed ennui. And it's certainly true that Emma regards all social functions as opportunities to display her better charms and talents. Yet Emma may be understood as Austen's portrayal of an exceptional individual constrained by a mediocre society.

Activity 31-4 (Editing 3 in Chapter 31 of *The Blair Handbook*)

31b Using the dictionary and thesaurus

31c Expanding your vocabulary

Using context and your knowledge of prefixes, suffixes, and roots, guess the meaning of italicized words in the following sentences. Then check the accuracy of your guesses by looking up the words in a dictionary.

1. Eunice acted as though she were a *conscript* when forced to play the role of Madame

   Bouvard in our production.

2. She would have preferred contributing in some *nondramatic* capacity

3. Although occasionally *immodest,* Madame Bouvard is still essentially a moral woman.

4. Because of the proximity of the furniture and the sets onstage, waltzing around requires

   a certain amount of *surefootedness.*

5. The script was the result of a collaborative writing project, so the real achievement lay

   in the *contexture.*

Activity 31-5 (Editing 4 in Chapter 31 of *The Blair Handbook*)

31d Considering connotations

Complete the following passage, choosing one of the two words in each set of parentheses. Be sure the words you choose have the connotations you want. More than one version is possible for some sentences.

As a girl, my grandmother worked in a textile mill. Recently she (revealed to/told) me

what it was like for her. Every morning she had to feed her (younger/youthful) brother and

sister breakfast and then take them to the house of Cousin Sophia, who looked after them.

My grandmother was at the (gates/portal) of the factory by 5:25 A.M. If an employee was

late, she would (forfeit/lose) half a day's pay. The work was (drab/tedious) and exhausting.

My grandmother had to (patrol/watch) and tend the same machine for hours on end, with

nothing to (distract/entertain) her but the whirring and clanking of the engines. Her lunch

hour was just fifteen minutes long, and she often (toiled/worked) sixteen hours a day.

Activity 31–6 (Editing 5 in Chapter 31 of *The Blair Handbook*)

31f Using standard idioms

Edit the following paragraph to make sure that words and expressions are used according to convention. More than one edited version is possible.

Just a few short years ago, computers were rare as chickens' teeth on college campuses. Students had to type their papers or write them with hand, just as they had for generations. Today, however; most of us either own a word processor or have access to one owned by our schools. This has had an enormous affect both on the process we use to create papers and on the papers themselves. Some students still think they can just sit down in front of a computer the night before a paper is due, flip a switch, and crank out a paper with no real work. Most of us, however, know the truth of the computer-era saying "Garbage in, garbage out." A computer can do some of the drudgery and can make problem solving more creative, but you still have to put your face to the grindstone to write a really good paper.

■ **Activity 31–7** (Editing 7 in Chapter 31 of *The Blair Handbook*)

31g Using slang, regionalisms, and colloquialisms sparingly

31h Using jargon carefully

Edit the following paragraph, making sure that slang and technical language are used only where appropriate. More than one edited version is possible.

Thirty percent of the students interviewed in the study said they owned personal computers and used them regularly to write papers. Many take basic precautions to safeguard their files, such as occasionally backing up on floppies. Most of these said they have learned through experience how important it is to take such steps. Seventy-five percent of those who own computers have trashed a file at one time or another, and almost everyone reported knowing at least one fellow hacker whose hard disk has crashed.

■ **Activity 31–8**

31i Using figurative language effectively

31j Eliminating clichés

Edit the following passage to improve the use of figurative language. More than one edited version is possible.

That first day of school was hot as a firecracker. Heat seemed to pour from the asphalt in invisible waves as I trudged my way to this new, unknown prison. I knew that, coming from the city, I was going to be like a square peg in a round hole at this hick town high school. I wanted to run away, to join the merchant marines, anything to escape the nine months of agony that I knew was ahead of me. Why had my parents insisted on moving to the middle of nowhere in the summer before my senior year? Did they want their only son to kick the bucket before his eighteenth birthday? By the time I reached Culpepper High, I was soaked with perspiration and as unhappy as a person could possibly be.

■ Activity 31–9

31i Using figurative language effectively

31j Eliminating clichés

Edit the following paragraph to improve the use of figurative language. More than one edited version is possible.

The tradition of giving up one's seat on a bus or train to elderly and disabled people has passed away. I ride the subway to and from school every day, along with lots of other people going to work or school. Everyone on the train is dog-tired, especially in the evening on the way home, and wants to sit down. Unfortunately, there just aren't enough seats for everyone. I have seen young, healthy people hurry in front of slower people, often elderly or disabled, to grab the last remaining seat. In this day and age, no one expects men to automatically give up their seats to women, but as a result, no one gives up a seat for anybody.

■ Activity 31–10 (Editing 8 in Chapter 31 of *The Blair Handbook*)

31i Using figurative language effectively

31j Eliminating clichés

Edit the following paragraph to improve the use figurative language. More than one edited version is possible.

Many people object to the television cartoon *The Simpsons* because they say it is over the top, but millions of children watch it with bated breath every week. Critics say shows like this are causing the American family to disintegrate and are teaching children that it is okay not to hit the books. They think that young people want to be like Bart Simpson, who is as proud as a peacock of being a bad student, and that the show is a stumbling block for students who want to be above par. I think it's crystal clear that children can tell the difference between television and reality. When they laugh at Bart talking back to his parents, they are just letting off steam because adults are always laying down the law.

■ Activity 31-11 (Editing 9 in Chapter 31 of *The Blair Handbook*)

Edit the following passage, making sure that each word is the best one possible. More than one edited version is possible.

If the nineties have been a golden era for home shopping channels, it has also been one for mail-order catalogs. In the past five years the number of catalogs delivered to American homes has tripled. Vendors compose not only old favorites such as L. L. Bean and discount electronics distributors, but also newer outfits that have been created merely to take advantage this trend. According to one survey, the average mail-order catalog junkie receives ten garb catalogs, nine catalogs for housewares and garden equipment, five catalogs for his or her favorite hobby, and six gift catalogs each month. And this doesn't even take into account the specialized catalogs that focus on children, pets, and any other earmark of a consumer's life that might result in a purchase or two. Mail-order companies sell each other their lists of suckers so once a consumer receives one catalog, chances are that he or she will be receiving catalogs to life.

■ ■ ■

Eliminating Biased Language

Edit the following passage to eliminate language that suggests any racial, ethnic, gender, or age bias. More than one edited version is possible.

Most people think that policemen and firemen have the most stressful of urban jobs, but statistics show that cabdrivers suffer more on-the-job stress than either of these two groups (Seligman, 192). A cabdriver puts himself at risk every hour he is on the streets, according to most of the drivers I interviewed.

Joe D'Amico is a typical Italian-American: friendly, boisterous, ready to talk your ear off no matter what the question. He's been driving a cab for five years and has been robbed three times, twice at gunpoint by drug dealer types, once at knifepoint by a well-dressed white man. "It's a jungle out there," D'Amico says. "Fighting traffic is bad enough, but wondering every time you pick up a passenger who's going to be sitting two feet behind you is worse."

Marla Crews, an attractive mother of three who has been driving a cab for two years, agrees. "I wouldn't be doing this if the money weren't good," says Ms. Crews. "I already have an ulcer from the day-to-day stress just in the short time I've been driving."

Senior citizen Jacob Matthews, a black man who is still capable and satisfied with the job after driving a cab for almost forty years, was the only dissenter: "When you drive a cab, you have to go with the flow. I enjoy my work because I don't let it get to me. And it's better than sitting on some assembly line."

Activity 32-2 (Editing 2 in Chapter 32 of *The Blair Handbook*)

32a Replacing stereotypes with specifics

32b Using labels carefully

Identify stereotypes in the following passages and describe the ways in which they may be thoughtless or offensive. If any useful information is conveyed by a particular passage, edit it to communicate the information in a way that is not offensive.

1. The biggest menace on our highways is teenagers and old folks.

2. No matter how reliable your housekeeper may seem, it's best not to give her a key to your house. It could easily end up in the hands of a drug-addicted grandson.

3. Children of recent immigrants are generally either underachievers or overachievers.

4. The husband in the movie is a typical accountant: bland, boring, and conventional. His flaky, astrology-obsessed wife is pure Californian.

5. The willingness of Japanese workers to value team effort above individual reward gives the companies they work for an unfair advantage in international trade.

Activity 32–3

32c Avoiding pronouns that may alienate readers

Edit the following passage to eliminate pronouns or sexist language that may offend readers. More than one edited version is possible.

Almost everyone who enters medical school expects that he will become a family practitioner when he graduates. By the time they graduate, however, the overwhelming majority of medical students have decided to specialize. The benefits of specialization are many. Some doctors are lured by the large salaries that specialists earn. They want their wives and children to be able to live in style. Many women doctors like the fact that patients' emergencies rarely disrupt a specialist's family life. But drawbacks exist as well. The number of nonspecialists has dropped so sharply that some communities find themselves without any family practitioners. What does a parent in such a community do when her child suddenly runs a fever? Whom does she call? In response to the growing problem, the government—encouraged by congressmen from those states with the greatest shortages—has begun to offer programs to encourage medical students to pursue careers in family practice. A student is given money toward medical school if he agrees to pursue a career in family practice when he graduates. Increasing numbers of students are taking this option, and many are finding that the personal rewards more than compensate for the smaller salary.

■ Activity 32–4 (Editing 4 in Chapter 32 of *The Blair Handbook*)

32   Eliminating biased language

Edit the following passage, eliminating any biased language that may be offensive to readers. More than one edited version is possible.

All of the old people at White Pines Residence agree that there couldn't be a better place for them to live. The modern residence has been designed to meet their every need, and in some ways it resembles a spa more than an old-age home. For one thing, the food is terrific. Every meal offers at least one exotic dish, always cooked to perfection. This isn't surprising, considering that the chef was born in Paris. In the medical area, facilities and services are first rate. A doctor is on call around the clock to provide care to all of the residents, many of whom suffer from cancer. With the handicapped in mind, doorways have been built that are wide enough for a cripple's wheelchair to pass through, and ramps are familiar sights, both inside and outside. Staff members have been carefully chosen for both their experience with old people and their personalities. They are all extremely popular with the residents. One of the best loved is a male nurse who always makes time in his busy schedule to read to the blind residents. Another nurse is a former actress; she has arranged for a local theater group to perform regularly at the residence. In addition, volunteers from the local college visit with the residents, providing them with companionship and friendship. Like so many old people, the residents at White Pines enjoy spending time with young people and telling stories about their youth. State-of-the art facilities are not cheap, however, and White Pines is no exception; the cost of the facility may explain the high percentage of Jewish residents. To judge from the level of satisfaction among the residents, however, it is money well spent.

■ ■ ■
Connecting Fused Sentences
and Comma Splices

Edit the following passage to eliminate fused sentences and comma splices. More than one edited version is possible.

Historians have made us aware that the Iroquois Indians of the northeastern United States had a form of government very much like the democracies of today however few people are aware of the important roles played by women in the Iroquois tribes. Iroquois women held important rights and responsibilities in many areas, including political life, social life, civil decisions, religious ceremonies, and land rights. Iroquois women had an important voice in public councils, they were free to make nominations just as the men were. Within the family, the Iroquois woman played roles still played by men in many cultures, she negotiated marriages and governed the household. The Iroquois mother had certain maternal rights. For example, it was up to the mother of a particular clan to decide which of the offspring would carry on the clan title. Similarly, the Iroquois woman held possession of lands and properties she could bequeath them to whomever she chose. In the case of civil decisions such as clan disputes over land, Iroquois women held important responsibilities. They acted as modern-day judges do, they ruled on who held rights to land and property. And finally, in religious life Iroquois women played important roles in various festivals and ceremonies. Some cultures still deny fundamental rights to women, years and years ago the Iroquois Indians were calling the earth their "mighty mother" and treating women with respect.

Activity 33-2 (Editing I in Chapter 33 of *The Blair Handbook*)

33a Using a comma and a coordinating conjunction

Edit each fused sentence or comma splice using a comma and a coordinating conjunction. More than one editing option is available to you.

1. The praise that David Halberstam has received for his nonfiction writing is due in large part to his blunt style he always says what he means.

2. He was critical of the media's involvement in the 1988 presidential election, he said so openly.

3. In his writing he not only identifies the point he is trying to make, he also proceeds to solidify and clarify it.

4. He leads the reader through his thought processes, rarely is any point unsubstantiated.

5. He feels strongly about his subjects he seems to become very involved with them.

■ Activity 33–3 (Editing 2 in Chapter 33 of *The Blair Handbook*)

33b Using a semicolon

Edit each fused sentence or comma splice using either a semicolon alone or a semicolon with a conjunctive adverb or transitional expression. More than one editing option is available to you.

1. John McPhee's "The Headmaster" focuses on Boyden's methods of running a boarding school, it includes several humorous anecdotes of how Boyden made Deerfield Academy a success.

2. Boyden is the only named character no one else shares the stage.

3. Throughout the story, McPhee's own voice is silent, he lets the anecdotes speak for themselves.

4. McPhee describes some of Boyden's unorthodox policies for example there were no formal rules.

5. McPhee does not merely state that Boyden's policies worked, instead he lets the reader infer this.

Activity 33–4 (Editing 3 in Chapter 33 of *The Blair Handbook*)

33c Using a colon

Edit each fused sentence or comma splice using a colon.

1. Ben and Jerry are known for their support of environmental causes, they recycle their plastic spoons and all recyclable paper trash.

2. The company is "one percent for peace," one percent of all sales goes toward supporting peacekeeping efforts worldwide.

3. They have an innovative way of generating business from time to time they give out free ice cream.

4. Ben and Jerry's is a great place to work, the co-workers are friendly, and sometimes employees get to take home free ice cream.

5. Ben and Jerry sought a location for their factory that would meet their specific demands, easy access to transportation, fresh water, and a high-quality work force were all important factors.

Activity 33–5 (Editing 4 in Chapter 33 of *The Blair Handbook*)

33d Writing separate sentences

Edit each fused sentence or comma splice by separating it into two sentences.

1. Thurgood Marshall, one of the most important figures in twentieth-century American life, died in 1993 he was eighty-four years old.

2. Marshall gained recognition from the 1954 Supreme Court decision *Brown* v. *Board of Education*, it was a landmark in American history.

3. Not everyone was happy with the decision that put an end to the "separate but equal" system of racial segregation, much turmoil followed.

4. Marshall was excluded from the all-white law school that later honored him, they named the library after him.

5. America was deep in the Great Depression when Marshall began his career as a lawyer times were very tough economically.

Activity 33-6 (Editing 5 in Chapter 33 of *The Blair Handbook*)

33e Subordinating one clause to the other

Edit the following passage to eliminate fused sentences and comma splices by subordinating clauses as appropriate. More than one edited version is possible.

Darkness falls the animals begin to settle down for the night. The horses all have their favorite places to sleep, they sleep standing. The chickens have already settled into the shed, occasionally they give off a muffled coo. The piglets playfully scampered all day now they lie quietly in a comfortable pile in the corner of their pen. Everything is quiet, little scratching, scurrying sounds can be heard from the feed room. The mice have come out, they believe they are the true owners of the barn. To a mouse a barn must resemble a cornucopia of hay, oats, and other delicacies, its other residents are all messy eaters. Three of the mice gnaw at the corner of a sack of rolled oats. The three are thinking of nothing but oats around the corner of the door creeps the cat.

■ **Activity 33–7** (Editing 6 in Chapter 33 of *The Blair Handbook*)

33f Rewriting the sentence as one independent clause

Edit each fused sentence or comma splice by making it a single independent clause. More than one editing option is available to you.

1. *Hamlet* is the most popular of Shakespeare's plays, more has been written about it than any other drama.

2. Shakespeare fused several similar plots, he created a new one that is just a little different.

3. One theme in the play is revenge another used is madness.

4. A third theme is crisis, it is created in the play by Hamlet's mother through her sin with Hamlet's uncle.

5. All three themes are familiar ones Shakespeare's blending of them makes them fascinating.

■ **Activity 33–8** (Editing 7 in Chapter 33 of *The Blair Handbook*)

33   Connecting fused sentences and comma splices

Edit the following passage to eliminate fused sentences and comma splices using any strategy discussed in this chapter.

Last year 169,574 people flew into or out of the airport, and a total of 7,215 flights arrived and departed, according to a recent report. On average, 2.3 people came to see off or to meet every passenger consequently, more than half a million people used the airport. Expanding the airport will generate more flights, more flights will bring more travelers and money into the region. Each traveler spends an average of $7 in the airport on goods and services, when parking and ground transportation is added, the total approaches $25. The report said that developing the local economy would benefit the area, it said that air travel would make traffic problems worse on roads around the airport. According to the report, expanding the airport offers many advantages, including providing jobs, making travel more convenient, and boosting the economy. However, the expansion plan faces some problems, it would cost $17 million and the new airport would have to be built on land that might be valuable as wetlands. Opponents of the airport expansion appeared before the port commission, saying that new runways would endanger the nesting grounds of several rare migratory birds. The Department of Environmental Quality studied the bird migration patterns it said that the fifteen acres of wetlands in question were home to at least nineteen different species. The Southeast Region Chamber of Commerce has supported the airport expansion, claiming that the plan could create dozens of new jobs, the chamber president called those jobs more important than a few ducks.

■ ■ ■

Eliminating Sentence Fragments

Edit the following passage to eliminate sentence fragments. More than one edited version is possible.

My experience as a camp counselor has taught me many lessons. The kind of lessons I cannot easily put into words. For two summers now I have worked as a counselor at a camp for children with learning disabilities. Each summer the entire staff gathers for a week of training at the end of June. After a few weeks of recovering from finals and the end of school. This training period is important. Because there is a lot to keep in mind when working with these children. Learning disabilities can be triggered by a long list of causes. Such as behavioral problems, visual or perceptual difficulties, or the strain of an unhappy life at home. To name just a few. That first week of training helps the counseling staff to keep these possible causes in mind and to be more sensitive to the problems each individual child might face.

I will always remember one nine-year-old boy named Johnny. Who was a camper during my first summer as a counselor. Johnny had trouble reading even the simplest sentences aloud. Every time he tried to read aloud his whole body would grow tense. And he would stumble painfully over every word. One day before reading class I had an idea. When it was Johnny's turn to read that day, I sat beside him. Gently rubbing his back as he began to read. It worked. Johnny's body relaxed, and he read an entire paragraph with only a few stumbles. When he finished he looked up at me with wide, surprised eyes. And grinned from ear to ear.

■ **Activity 34–2** (Editing I in Chapter 34 of *The Blair Handbook*)

34a Recognizing and editing phrase fragments

Edit the following passage to eliminate any fragments, making small changes in wording or punctuation that are necessary for smooth reading. More than one edited version is possible.

There he stood. In the middle of the public square. Speaking at the top of his lungs about the end of the world. After two or three hours in the hot sun, he rested. Sat down in the shade of the clock tower. He opened his satchel and took out his lunch. A banana. A small can of apple juice. Three cookies and a wedge of cheese. I walked over to talk to him. He looked me right in the eye. For a long moment. Then spoke: "Have a cookie."

■ **Activity 34–3** (Editing 2 in Chapter 34 of *The Blair Handbook*)

34b Recognizing and editing dependent clause fragments

Edit the following paragraph to eliminate dependent clause fragments. More than one edited version is possible.

Despite the fact that doctors take an oath to protect life. Many physicians believe they should be allowed to help patients who want to commit suicide. They want to do whatever they can to ease the pain of death for those who are suffering. Because they believe people should be able to die with dignity. In Europe, although euthanasia is not legal, it is becoming more accepted in some countries, such as the Netherlands. Which has one of the most liberal policies in the world. There, specific guidelines allow a doctor to assist in the suicide of a patient who is terminally ill. As long as the patient requests it.

■ **Activity 34–4** (Editing 5 in Chapter 34 of *The Blair Handbook*)

Edit the following passage to eliminate sentence fragments. Make any small changes in wording that are needed for smooth reading. More than one edited version is possible.

Ferninand le Menthe Morton was born in New Orleans to a Creole family. Although he took classical piano lessons, he fell in love with another kind of music. Jazz and blues. Which he heard in the part of town called Storyville. In Chicago in the 1920s, he got a recording contract with RCA. He made some records and began calling himself "Jelly Roll." He claimed to have invented jazz. By himself. George G. Wolfe wrote a musical about his life. Called *Jelly's Last Jam* and written as though looking back from the moment of his death.

At the end of his life, Morton came face to face with the contributions of other blacks to jazz. Which he had denied all his life. He also had to confront the heritage he shared with black musicians. He eventually came to accept and understand them. Although he had always thought of himself, a Creole, as different from blacks.

■ ■ ■

Selecting Correct Verbs

Edit the following passage to eliminate incorrect verb forms. More than one edited version is possible.

Many people think that winter is the most dangerous season for bacterial infections. But summertime can be dangerous, too. If you are careful, though, you can avoid these summertime dangers. The first place to have watched for disease-causing bacteria in the summer is the water. Generally, pools are carefully monitor. But lakes and ponds were another story. Severe stomach upset can be bringed on by bacteria such as salmonella and shigella. These bacteria may lay waiting in natural bodies of water. Be careful not to ingest water if you swam in lakes and ponds. Experts recommend that you contact the local health department if you are unsure about a particular body of water. Be careful also with food in the summer. Disease-causing bacteria such as salmonella and listeria can create problems if food were not handled properly. For example, you should not leave foods like tuna salad or potato salad setting on your kitchen counter for very long. Similarly, you should not leave foods like these laying in a hot car. Meat can have been especially dangerous. If it is froze, meat should be thawn in the refrigerator. After it is thawed, it should be cooked and ate right away.

Activity 35–2

35a Understanding verb forms
35b Using standard verb forms

Edit the following sentences using the correct -s and -ed forms and forms of irregular verbs.

1. Sheehy share experiences that focus on concerns common to all people.

2. She start as a fashion editor and then writed features for a major New York newspaper.

3. She also contribute to magazines as an editor and freelance writer before her career as a novelist begun.

4. Although her first novels receive mixed reviews, she persevere and hope to publish more novels.

5. Her novels is about common human experiences.

Activity 35–3

35a Understanding verb forms
35b Using standard verb forms

Edit the following passage, using the correct -s and -ed forms and forms of irregular verbs.

The waiter setted down two hot chocolates topped with whipped cream at the table where we sat. The bell over the door rung repeatedly as a steady stream of hungry diners enter. The winter sun shined brightly through the large glass panes next to us as we drunk our hot chocolate. I be resting comfortably in the corner of the booth when suddenly I beholded the woman at the next table as she sprung up and walk toward the door. I gave my companion a questioning look and asked, "What do you think she meaned by that?"

Activity 35–4 (Editing 2 in Chapter 35 of *The Blair Handbook*)

35c Using auxiliary verbs

Complete the following sentences by supplying an appropriate auxiliary verb in each blank. Some sentences may have more than one possible answer.

1. Children were taught the rudiments of education while they _____ receiving religious

    instruction.

2. After the home _____ destroyed by a fire around the turn of the century, Wheeler hoped

    that enough money _____ be raised to build a new center.

3. A new home _____ built where up to seventy children _____ reside while they waited,

    hoping that they _____ be adopted.

4. Around World War I, the administration provided agricultural training to the children so

    that they _____ grow their own food.

5. In the 1950s, the administration decided to hire social workers and psychologists who

    _____ further serve the children's needs.

6. The center _____ still growing today, and family therapy sessions _____ begun.

■ Activity 35-5

35a Understanding verb forms
35b Using standard verb forms
35c Using auxiliary verbs

Edit the following passage, using correct verb forms.

As many cities throughout the world struggles to deal with increasing traffic and the problems of pollution that accompanies it, Amsterdam has putted in place a plan that could eventually ban all cars from the city. Parking spaces is virtually nonexistent, and the streets can be very difficult to negotiate in a car as they become narrower and narrower. The sidewalks has been widened for pedestrians, and new bicycle paths are being built. Other cities in Europe must no doubt be watching to see how successful Amsterdam's plan be before they adopt similar policies. But not everyone be happy with the changes. Walking, cycling, shopping, people watching, street music, and other street events may be booming, but, critics wonders, at what cost? Their main concern are how the economy will be affected. Will businesses move out of the city, unable to do business without buses, trucks, and automobiles? They argues that the plan's proponents must realize that quality of life mean more than just clean air and less noise.

■ Activity 35-6

35d Understanding verb tenses

Edit the following passage, changing all present-tense verbs into the corresponding past-tense forms.

For several years the university has been requiring incoming students to purchase a computer. Some students are unhappy with the decision; tuition and room and board are already too expensive. Others find computers in every dorm room dehumanizing. But there are many arguments in favor of computers as well. Many students at other schools regularly use computers to write their papers, and at some schools they are sending mail and consulting with their professors by computer. Computers are also useful, of course, for playing video games. Ultimately, those students who are opposed to the idea just have to accept that computers have become a fact of life.

■ Activity 35-7 (Editing 3 in Chapter 35 of *The Blair Handbook*)

35d Understanding verb tenses

Edit the following passage twice, changing the verbs first to the present tense and then to the future tense.

For one week at the beginning of each semester sororities opened their houses to prospective members. The women took their best dresses off their hangers and carefully painted on their makeup. Along with frozen hair went frozen smiles. Hundreds of young women moved from house to house where they were looked over and judged. For some women this was an exciting time; for others it was humiliating and degrading.

Activity 35–8

35e Using the present tense for habitual or future actions

Edit the following passage, using the literary present tense consistently.

Each week in the tutorial following the lecture we will discuss a different dialogue of Plato. This week we are discussing *The Symposium.* In this dialogue, which Plato wrote in the fourth century B.C., a group of Athenian men gathered at a dinner party and took turns talking about what they thought love was. One of the guests is Socrates, whose speech was actually the centerpiece of the work. The speakers who precede Socrates also contribute interesting points, including Aristophanes, who writes comedies in real life. He expressed his view that love is more than physical desire, an idea that Socrates comes back to later in the dialogue. Next week we will read Plato's *Republic.*

Activity 35–9 (Editing 4 in Chapter 35 of *The Blair Handbook*)

35f Using verb tenses in appropriate sequence

Edit the following passage, using appropriate verb tenses and putting them in a logical sequence. More than one edited version is possible.

Many people thought that it will never happen, but Los Angeles has finally opened a subway system. Perhaps you imagine that the name L.A. will never be associated with public transit, because it was practically synonymous with the word *automobile.* When questioned, some people say that the new system, although it is modest so far, can be a turning point for the city. If you have visited New York City which has more than 450 stations and hundreds of miles of tracks, you will realize that the new system is quite small. On opening day, supporters of the new system had said that they hoped to have put the city's dollars toward building stations rather than freeways.

Activity 35-10

35h Using the subjunctive mood

Edit the following sentences, using subjunctive verb forms wherever appropriate. Circle the number of any correct sentence.

1. Phil wished that he was going somewhere else tonight.

2. If he had already made plans he would not have to attend.

3. He could have made other plans if he would have thought about it earlier.

4. As the door opened, Phil put a smile on his face as though he was happy to be there.

5. He would have worn a tuxedo if he had known that formal dress were required.

Activity 35-11 (Editing 5 in Chapter 35 of *The Blair Handbook*)

35h Using the subjunctive mood

Edit the following passage, using subjunctive verb forms wherever appropriate.

He opens the refrigerator door and catches sight of the single slice of birthday cake. If only it was not the last piece of cake! A voice inside his head demands that he does not eat it. "If it is not my birthday, I should not eat the last piece of cake," he thinks. But a second voice insists that he helps himself. "If it was my birthday, I would not mind if someone else eats it," he reasons. His conscience prevails. He sighs, closes the refrigerator door, and wishes that he has never even come into the kitchen.

Activity 35–12 (Editing 6 in Chapter 35 of *The Blair Handbook*)

Edit the following passage, using the correct form, tense, and mood of each verb. More than one edited version is possible.

In the early years of this century, the Constitution stated that women cannot vote. Suffragists wished that every woman citizen was able to vote and they strived to amend the Constitution so that no state can deny any citizen the right to vote on account of sex. For this to happen, the Constitution required that three-quarters of the states were in favor of the amendment. Many of the arguments against women's suffrage strike us as absurd now. Some people argued that women do not understand the business world; others said that the cost of elections will go up. If women would get the vote, some worried, next they would want to hold office. Some felt that a woman is represented by her husband and that when he voted it was as though she was voting. Some also feared that a vote for women will be a step toward feminism, which many people consider a radical and dangerous idea.

Making Subjects and Verbs Agree

Edit the following passage to make subjects and verbs agree. More than one edited version is possible.

Those in favor of government funding for the arts argues that without the arts, civilizations would cease to exist. But without the sciences, civilizations would not exist in the first place. All important civilizations, from ancient China and the Roman Empire to America in the twentieth century, has acknowledged the importance of scientific research. To ignore the important advances of science are dangerous for a society. Today, the economics of scientific funding is very complex. Determining which of various research projects get funded is difficult. The number of projects receiving funding are limited by today's weak economy. Much of today's funding goes toward applied science. Included in this category is cancer research and advances in industrial technology. Millions of dollars is spent on applied scientific research each year. But the parent of applied research projects are pure science. Research on a particular plant species or experimenting with subatomic particles is an example of pure science. Data from pure scientific research forms the base on which applied research build. Many people acknowledge the importance of funding for applied research. But few recognizes how crucial pure scientific research continues to be. A new treatment for disease or an advance in computer technology never happen without the necessary groundwork in pure science. Because we can see direct results, applied science sometimes seems more important and more exciting than pure science. But neither are enough alone. International Business Machines (IBM) are important. But so are the

calculations and theories of a researcher in pure mathematics.

■ **Activity 36–2**

36a Ignoring words between subject and verb
36b Finding the subject when it follows the verb
36c Finding the subject of a linking verb

Edit the following sentences to make each verb agree with its subject. Take special care when identifying the subject. Circle the number of any sentence that is correct.

1. A debate, especially for a candidate who is low in the polls, matter considerably.

2. The public's perception of the candidates' performances make a huge difference in an election.

3. Students of the political process has long been fascinated by the impact of the debate on the 1960 election.

4. Richard M. Nixon and John F. Kennedy, each a respected politician, was intelligent and articulate.

5. Many political analysts believe that the debates were the deciding factor in the election.

6. There was many people who thought that Nixon looked bad on television.

7. Others, who listened to the debates on the radio only, has said that Nixon argued more effectively.

8. During the 1992 campaign, the format of the debates were discussed at length.

9. Bill Clinton, along with the two other candidates, George Bush and Ross Perot, were on the stage three times.

10. There was questions from members of the audience in the second debate.

Activity 36–3 (Editing I in Chapter 36 of *The Blair Handbook*)

36a Ignoring words between subject and verb

36b Finding the subject when it follows the verb

36c Finding the subject of a linking verb

Edit the following passage to make verbs agree with their subjects. Take special care when identifying the subject.

Canada, along with Europe and many cities in the United States, have found great success in curbing the spread of AIDS through needle exchange programs. These kinds of programs is an effective way to slow down the spread of the virus among intravenous drug users. There are many who are convinced that providing addicts with clean needles does not result in increased drug use. Others, who think that such programs encourage the use of drugs and sends the wrong message to young people, remains firmly opposed. To this group, free needles and free drug use is one and the same. But, supporters of the idea points out, one of the most important parts of needle exchange programs are educating users about the dangers of sharing needles. After all, intravenous drug users is a segment of the population with an especially high rate of HIV infection, which causes AIDS. And the spread of AIDS and other infectious diseases are a matter of concern for all people.

Activity 36–4 (Editing 2 in Chapter 36 of *The Blair Handbook*)

36d Making verbs agree with subjects joined by <u>and</u>

36e Making verbs agree with subjects joined by <u>or</u> or <u>nor</u>

Edit the following sentences to make verbs agree with their compound subjects. Circle the number of any sentence that is correct.

1. Neither the butler nor the chauffeur behave oddly in front of the police.

2. Each man and woman is under suspicion.

3. Not only the time of death but also the choice of weapons figure into the equation.

4. A telephone call or a message sent beyond the premises are forbidden during the investigation.

5. Motive and alibi each matters in an investigation.

6. The inspector and the coroner disagrees.

7. Neither overeating nor lack of sleep typically cause death.

8. Both strychnine and cyanide was found in the doctor's bag.

9. The sum and substance of the investigation are interrogation.

10. Not only the gardener but also the cook are a possible suspect.

■ Activity 36–5

36f Making verbs agree with collective nouns

Edit each sentence, selecting the verb from the parentheses that agrees with the collective subject. Think about how the meaning changes depending on whether you select a singular or a plural verb.

1. The office improvement committee (decide/decides) to recycle most of the waste paper in

    the office.

2. The clerical staff (meet/meets) to discuss the procedures.

3. The group (seem/seems) determined to recycle 70 percent of the garbage.

4. A number of unsuccessful attempts (take/takes) place.

5. Top management (are/is) completely behind the efforts of the committee.

■ Activity 36–6

36g Making verbs agree with indefinite pronouns

Edit the following sentences to make verbs agree with indefinite pronoun subjects. Circle the number of any sentence that is correct.

1. All of the employees thinks that the hours are too long.

2. Much of their dissatisfaction result from their low salaries and poor benefits.

3. Neither of the women executives have been promoted in ten years.

4. Of the profits earned in the last quarter, more is slated for research and development

    than for improving working conditions.

5. With the salary freeze, none of the clerical staff is getting more money this year.

Activity 36-7 (Editing 3 in Chapter 36 of *The Blair Handbook*)

36f Making verbs agree with collective nouns

36g Making verbs agree with indefinite pronouns

36h Making verbs agree with <u>who</u>, <u>which</u>, and <u>that</u>

Edit the following subjects to make verbs agree with collective noun subjects, indefinite pronoun subjects, and relative pronoun subjects. Circle the number of any sentence that is correct.

1. The pictures in the exhibit, which are open every night, feature children from Third

    World countries.

2. Many of the children photographed in Mexico was casualties of the earthquake.

3. Most people find that it is the look of sadness on their faces that are most moving.

4. The best of the photographers, who spend three months every year in Southeast Asia,

    has won numerous awards.

5. The museum committee has a variety of opinions on the exhibit.

6. Adding photography exhibits to the museum was one of many good ideas of the curator,

    who is herself a photographer.

7. Much of her energy are spent finding good exhibits and soliciting contributions from

    patrons.

■ Activity 36-8

36i Making verbs agree with subjects that refer to amounts

Edit the following sentences to make verbs agree with subjects that refer to amounts. Circle the number of any sentence that is correct.

1. They are especially hungry because seven hours has elapsed since their last meal.

2. Half the restaurants on this street caters to businesspeople.

3. Three-quarters of the items on the menu has meat in them.

4. Half the guests is vegetarian.

5. Ninety percent of their choices is unavailable.

6. Usually they go to restaurants where one hundred percent of the dishes is meatless.

7. A dollar and a quarter are not much to pay for a soft drink.

8. Thirty dollars are more than he expected to pay for a main course.

9. Twenty dollars are all she can afford.

10. Half her money is being saved for a taxi to take her home after dinner.

Activity 36–9

36i Making verbs agree with subjects that refer to amounts

36j Using singular verbs with noun phrases or clauses

Edit the following sentences to make verbs agree with their subjects that refer to amounts, noun phrase subjects, or clause subjects. Circle the number of any sentence that is correct.

1. That she might be able to help suffering animals have contributed to her decision to be

    a vet.

2. Immunizing cats and dogs against rabies protect humans as well as their pets.

3. Two hundred dollars are a lot to pay for a routine examination.

4. Half the cat owners in the United States believe that declawing is inhumane.

5. To care for their four-footed companions are the responsibility of all animal lovers.

Activity 36–10 (Editing 4 in Chapter 36 of *The Blair Handbook*)

36j Using singular verbs with noun phrases or clauses
36k Using singular verbs with titles and words used as words
36l Using singular verbs with singular subjects that end in -s
36m Using singular verbs with troublesome plurals

Edit the following sentences to make verbs agree with their noun phrase or noun clause subjects, subjects that are titles or words used as words, or troublesome singular or plural subjects. Circle the number of any sentence that is correct.

1. Politics are not a field that I find interesting, but I do enjoy my world literature course.

2. Dostoyevsky's *Crime and Punishment* are exactly the sort of novel I would choose to read

    on my own.

3. That a young man would commit a murder for the reasons Dostoyevsky describes

    seems unthinkable to me.

4. To make interesting contributions to the weekly class discussions are one of my goals.

5. *Witticisms* are what I would like my classmates to call my comments.

Activity 36–11

36k Using singular verbs with titles and words used as words

Edit the following sentences to make verbs agree with their subjects. Circle the number of any sentence that is correct.

1. Jane Smiley's *Ordinary Love and Goodwill* are in a display case at the front of the store.

2. *Monkeys* are what the parents affectionately call their children in Susan Minot's first novel, which is also on sale.

3. Dostoyevsky's *Crime and Punishment*, which explore the complex psychology of human character, is sold out.

4. Alex Haley's *Roots* was made into a television miniseries.

5. Barnes and Noble also have these titles available.

Activity 36–12

36l Using singular verbs with singular subjects that end in ‑s

36m Using singular verbs with troublesome plurals

Edit the following sentences to make verbs agree with their troublesome singular and plural subjects. Circle the number of any sentence that is correct.

1. There is no single criterion for developing an economic plan.

2. Current data suggests that tax increases will be required to reduce the deficit.

3. The news are not good for those who expected to pay less.

4. Demographics are an important tool in developing a fair plan.

5. The media describes the new plan as "strong medicine."

6. Telecommunications are the name of the game in getting the message across.

7. The medium of television is where most people get their news.

8. Existing statistics indicates that spending cuts will also be necessary.

9. Advanced mathematics are helpful in understanding the new tax schedule.

Activity 36–13 (Editing 5 in Chapter 36 of *The Blair Handbook*)

Edit the following passage to make verbs agree with their subjects. More than one edited version is possible.

The county employees and volunteers who run the prison education program focuses on illiteracy. Statistics shows that among prison inmates nationwide, some 60 percent is illiterate, and neither substance abuse programs nor vocational training seem as effective as literacy education in limiting the return of repeat offenders. The core of the program, therefore, are reading and writing skills. Each employee and volunteer go through a three-week training program in literacy education. If they can demonstrate sufficiently high reading levels, inmates may also train to become tutors; by doing so, most earns points toward early probation. Tutoring for all participants takes place not only one on one but also in groups, and there is within each group inmates at various levels of reading proficiency. Even inmates who have never achieved any academic success learns without feeling intimidated. Current data shows a high rate of success.

■ ■ ■
Using Adjectives and Adverbs Correctly

■ Activity 37-1

Edit the following passage, using adjectives and adverbs correctly. More than one edited version is possible.

More and more people are becoming aware that Alzheimer's disease is a real serious problem for our society. Not hardly anyone will go through life without knowing someone with this disease. In the United States, as many as two million people over the age of sixty-five may have Alzheimer's disease. It is even more commoner among people over the age of eighty. Alzheimer's disease is one of the most common and least understood diseases known today. Researchers have identified two different types of Alzheimer's disease. The first type occurs in people over sixty-five and develops more slowly. In the second type, which occurs in people under sixty-five, the symptoms of the disease develop most quickly. People with Alzheimer's disease usually go through several different stages. In the early stages of the disease, patients often seem quite healthily. But by the time they reach the latter stages, most Alzheimer's patients can no longer care for themselves. In the final stages of the disease, many patients simply lie curled up in bed. The family members of people with Alzheimer's disease sometimes feel badly and blame themselves. But the disease is no one's fault. Doctors have not identified one most absolute cause of Alzheimer's disease. But research into the disease continues, and doctors hope that one day less people will have to suffer with this disease.

Activity 37–2 (Editing I in Chapter 37 of *The Blair Handbook*)

37a Choosing adjectives or adverbs

Edit the following sentences, using an adjective or an adverb when each is needed.

1. Measuring correct is the most important part of woodworking.

2. You have to measure real carefully, but your care is likely to pay off in the end.

3. For fine work, measure close. Use a pencil that marks clean.

4. Then you have to cut straight and true. Leave just a part of your mark showing, and the piece should fit perfect.

5. Any good woodworker can give you handily suggestions like these.

Activity 37–3 (Editing 2 in Chapter 37 of *The Blair Handbook*)

37b Using adjectives after linking verbs

Edit the following sentences, using adjectives and adverbs correctly after linking verbs. Circle the number of any sentence that is correct.

1. The coach sounds odd philosophical about the team's loss.

2. The players all seemed sadly disappointed.

3. How can they become happily?

4. The other team looked really nicely in their new uniforms and they played good enough to win the game.

5. The winners feel excitedly about their victory. All agree that even after a friendly game victory tastes deliciously.

Activity 37–4 (Editing 3 in Chapter 37 of *The Blair Handbook*)

37c Choosing between commonly confused modifiers

37d Avoiding double negatives

Edit the following passage, using the correct form of any commonly confused modifier and correcting any double negatives.

Things have been going real bad for the homeless in recent weeks. First, the city shut its main shelter. Later, a charity soup kitchen ran out of money. Every year the city seems to have more needy people and less dollars to help them. A more comprehensive program would mean less women and children sleeping on the street. Many of these people cannot hardly read or write good enough to get a job that pays good. With only a shelter to live in it's hard for them to feel well about themselves. They eat bad and they sleep bad, so it isn't no wonder that they feel bad too.

Activity 37–5

37d Avoiding double negatives

Edit the following sentences, eliminating any double negatives. Some sentences can be edited in more than one way. Circle the number of any sentence that is correct.

1. They don't have no idea of the side effects of anabolic steroids. About the many dangers of these powerful drugs they haven't heard nothing.

2. No matter what athletes may want to believe, it just isn't true that steroids cause no physical problems.

3. It's not as if don't have no psychological effects either.

4. There are hardly no parts of the body that can't be affected in one way or another.

5. It doesn't make no sense for the family members of athletes to ignore the warning signs of steroid use.

▊ Activity 37–6

37e Using comparatives and superlatives correctly

Edit the following sentences, using comparatives and superlatives correctly. Some sentences can be edited in more than one way. Circle the number of any sentence that is correct.

1. Computers can do many things, but the amazingest thing they can do is connect you with huge banks of data.

2. With an on-line data service you can make more better use of your computer.

3. Compared to browsing in a library, using an on-line data service is usually the best choice.

4. For finding baseball statistics, Supreme Court opinions, and medical journal articles, a service is more effective.

5. The most fastest way to research a subject is to search books, newspapers, and magazine articles for keywords.

6. For example, you could use "Control Data Corp." and "stock" as keywords to find out why the company's stock was doing more bad this year than last year.

7. A most unique on-line service is offered by some libraries.

8. The most quickest way to call up the card catalog is with your home computer.

9. Of course, you can waste time browsing, but having no access at all seems like the worser choice.

10. You'll have more better access to the information by using a computer, and in less time.

Activity 37–7 (Editing 4 in Chapter 37 of *The Blair Handbook*)

37e Using comparatives and superlatives correctly

Edit the following passage, using the correct comparative and superlative forms of adjectives and adverbs. More than one edited version is possible.

How do American students compare with students in other countries? In general, studies show that Americans do worser on tests. Scores on SATs and other standardized tests have been dropping more steadilier over the past decade in the United States. Perhaps we need to take a more closer look at what can be done to make our nation's young people gooder students. Perhaps it is time to admit that the more traditional methods of teaching may not be most perfect. To perform more well, students need to learn more than mere memorization skills; they have to learn the bestest way to study and how best to apply what they learn. With a new approach, perhaps students will find that learning takes lesser time and can even be funner.

Activity 37–8 (Editing 5 in Chapter 37 of *The Blair Handbook*)

Edit the following passage, using adjectives and adverbs correctly. More than one edited version is possible.

The fall leaves that had looked so colorfully had turned a more duller color and fallen from the trees weeks ago, leaving the woods grayer and more lonelier. The most sharpest, bitterest wind blew against me as I walked down the dirt road. I had to admit that I was likely to feel badly tomorrow. My hands felt warmly inside my woolen gloves, but I didn't have no hat. My ears felt raw, and the inside of my head throbbed bad.

I felt happier when I saw the large red building with its well-maintained outbuildings. The air smelled pungently: manure, feed, and animal smells were mixed together indistinguishable. I went over to the horse stalls in the barn, where real fragrant wood chips covered the dirt floor, strewn there to absorb the odors of the barn. The horses, covered up good in their colorful blankets seemed peaceful in their stalls. The warm air felt heavenly and, exhaustedly, I unzipped my jacket and sat down on the floor. I didn't know of no better place to get off my feet and rest for a while.

■ ■ ■

Positioning Modifiers Carefully

Edit the following passage to eliminate incorrectly placed modifiers. More than one edited version is possible.

One of the reasons I love swimming is that it makes me feel just strong. The farther I get into my thirty-six laps, the tougher I feel. Instead of spending my energy, it's being multiplied. The thoughts that go through my mind, even though I know this is just the effect of endorphins, are fabulous. Normally, I mean, my body image is something like this: I'm a wreck. But in the pool, I become the greatest undiscovered athlete of the decade—maybe even of the century. My body is uniquely and perfectly designed to execute this sport! People are moving over to the slow lane because they want to stay out of my way! Then another thing I love about swimming kicks in—my mind is completely free to willy-nilly follow these trains of thought wherever they lead. I can engage in daydreaming completely guilt-free. The two people standing at the end of the pool become the swim coaches. They are admiring my endurance and the efficiency of my stroke. Soon they are going to come over and recruit me for their team. They are Olympic talent-scouting coaches better yet. When I tell them the only time I have swum competitively was in the third grade, they refuse to believe me. "It just isn't possible," they say. I leave these fantasies in my gym bag, nearly always with my goggles and swimsuit. But I have a great time while I am inside them.

Activity 38–2 (Editing I in Chapter 38 of *The Blair Handbook*)

38a Repositioning misplaced modifiers

Edit the following passage, moving any misplaced modifiers. More than one edited version is possible.

Most people assume that black bears hibernate all winter incorrectly. During the winter, although sleeping deeply, a true state of hibernation is not achieved by black bears. Their body temperature only drops a little, and one can wake up just a black bear with a little effort. Preparing to sleep for several months, a very large amount of food is eaten by the bears. This way, they can store fat and feed off it all winter while they are sleeping. The female surprisingly gives birth to her young at this time.

Activity 38–3

38a Repositioning misplaced modifiers

Edit the following sentences, making sure that all modifiers are correctly placed. More than one edited version is possible.

1. He took several questions from journalists standing at the podium.

2. The president spoke for a few minutes to reporters on overstaffed army bases.

3. The president then promised to help Somalia feed its starving people at the press conference.

4. He denied trying to avoid the issue emphatically.

5. Leaving the room, one last question detained the president for a moment longer.

■ Activity 38–4

38b Placing limiting modifiers carefully

Edit the following passage to correct the placement of limiting modifiers. More than one edited version is possible.

Some students only attend college as a way to get a good job. They understand the connection that lies between education and earning potential perfectly. They don't see that there are simply other reasons to go to college. A handful seem just to think that learning for its own sake is enough. Most don't even see that one year spent at college will enrich their lives. Imagine what just four can do!

■ Activity 38–5

38b Placing limiting modifiers carefully

Edit the following sentences to correct the placement of limiting modifiers. Circle the number of any sentence that is correct.

1. She knows only how hard it is for me to be there on time. No one else does.

2. I understand that my walking in late bothers the others perfectly.

3. My bus merely runs every fifty minutes after 8:00 A.M.

4. I cannot simply make an earlier bus.

5. Why can't buses just run a bit more often?

■ Activity 38–5

38c Clarifying squinting modifiers

Edit the following sentences to connect the placement of squinting modifiers. Some sentences can be edited in more than one way. Circle the number of any sentence that is correct.

1. The newspaper that they read daily has an easy puzzle.

2. The Sunday paper's puzzle is more fun for them both because it is more challenging.

3. The words that are left blank invariably are extremely obscure.

4. The dictionary that they consult rarely is helpful.

5. The puzzles that they complete usually have no errors.

■ Activity 38–6

38c Clarifying squinting modifiers

Edit the following passage, correcting any squinting modifiers. More than one version is possible.

Two of us who commute between Washington and New York regularly meet for breakfast on the train. The train that we take usually makes no local stops. Menus that are handed out occasionally feature daily specials. Large mugs are given to us both for coffee and for tea. The bagel that I order always is still warm when I eat it. The jostling motion that the train makes frequently cause our drinks to spill.

Activity 38–7 (Editing 2 in Chapter 38 of *The Blair Handbook*)

38d Eliminating dangling modifiers

Edit the following passage, clarifying squinting modifiers and eliminating dangling modifiers. More than one edited version is possible.

Examining the patient death rates of more than fifty doctors, the results were compared by a panel to a statistical average. Having a better than average rate, a minus score was entered for those doctors. A positive score was entered for those who had worse than average rates. Consisting of only the doctors with positive scores, the panel released a list of names to a local newspaper. After reading the article, a protest was lodged by the county medical society. Doctors who criticized the study strongly argued that the scoring was biased.

■ Activity 38–8

38d Eliminating dangling modifiers

Edit the following sentences to eliminate any dangling modifiers. Some sentences can be edited in more than one way. Circle the number of any sentence that is correct.

1. Suffering hundreds of thousands of casualties, the armies of the Union experienced great hardships.

2. After putting an end to slavery and the agrarian way of life in the South, northern industry prospered.

3. Causing unprecedented death and destruction, more than 600,000 people died in the war.

4. Based on the plantation system, the South saw its economy change after the war.

5. Fighting for opposite causes, independence was sought by the South and restoration of the Union was desired by the North.

6. Having irreconcilable political differences, the conflict focused on whether slavery should be allowed in the new western states.

7. Having been granted the authority by Congress, over half a million men were recruited by Lincoln.

8. Having seceded from the Union, Jefferson Davis was elected provisional president of the Confederate states.

9. As the world's major cotton exporter, financial support was expected from abroad by the South.

10. Staying neutral in the conflict, there was no assistance from Britain and France.

Activity 38–9 (Editing 3 in Chapter 38 of *The Blair Handbook*)

38e Moving disruptive modifiers

Edit the following passage, moving disruptive modifiers for easier reading. More than one edited version is possible.

The writers and editors at *The New Yorker* use specific tactics to effectively fire their information at a very specific audience—educated middle- and upper-class individuals who work and play in New York City. The authors attempt through skillful use of sophisticated vocabulary, varied and complex sentence structure, and stimulating content to capture this readership. Their methods have in almost all instances given the readers what they want, namely the greatest amount of information in the fewest number of words. The magazine has been able to very easily fill, in the world of the written word, a niche. Its pages can be said to be brimming with well-documented material. It has become, for its comments regarding world issues, hints on the latest happenings in the Big Apple, and lighthearted quips, well regarded.

■ Activity 38–10

38e Moving disruptive modifiers

Edit the following sentences, moving disruptive modifiers for easier reading. Some sentences can be edited in more than one way. Circle the number of any sentence that is correct.

1. His books are the result of many years spent collecting data for a management consulting firm.

2. His approach is to factually relay his information.

3. His ability to thoroughly research and interview is topped only by his ability to logically organize the story line.

4. In The One-Minute Manager, Peters makes the point that, by selecting a qualified staff, a manager is able to significantly reduce his or her workload.

5. When subordinates have been properly and carefully, so that their work speaks for itself, chosen, there is no need to constantly review their work.

6. If a manager trusted their ability enough to hire them, now he or she should trust their ability to successfully produce results.

7. Peters has, with his sharp mind, managed to effectively distill the fundamental attributes of excellence down to eight major points.

8. Some people have criticized Peters's approach as too simplistic because he limits the analysis of business organizations to only eight dimensions.

9. The foundation of The Search for Excellence is the research efforts that Peters over the past twenty-five years for a management consulting firm conducted.

10. His second book, A Passion for Excellence, was able in its first four weeks on the bookstore shelves to realize sales of over 250,000.

■ Activity 38–11 (Editing 4 in Chapter 38 of *The Blair Handbook*)

Edit the following passage, eliminating dangling, disruptive, and squinting modifiers. More than one edited version is possible.

Striking millions of Americans, some people only are afflicted by insomnia occasionally, while other people live with it for several years. Having experienced mild, occasional sleeplessness, your insomnia shouldn't be considered a major concern. The causes from which it seem most often are quite simple. Having something troubling or exciting on your mind, exerting too much physical or mental activity before bedtime, having a mild fever, drinking too much caffeine, or eating a heavy meal, sleeplessness might occur. Changing your schedule or surroundings, insomnia can also result. The way to best ensure a good night's sleep is to consistently follow a few simple steps. Try to go to bed at the same time very night. Sleep on a comfortable bed in a dark room. Realizing that it is still, after twenty minutes, hard to fall asleep, it is helpful for you to get up and do something, such a read, until you feel drowsy. And remember to always avoid caffeine and heavy foods as well as strenuous activity before bedtime.

■ ■ ■

Making Pronouns and Antecedents Agree

Edit the following passage to make all pronouns agree with their antecedents. More than one edited version is possible.

Each of us has our own oddities. One of mine is a certain fondness for cows. It started on a walk one day, when I passed a field where a herd of cows was grazing, enclosed by a split-rail fence. Each cow and calf occupied their own square of grass, a long way off from the road—all but one the them, which was right by the fence. This is my chance to see a cow close up, I thought. As I came nearer, I saw why the cow was there all alone—their head was stuck in the fence! Poor thing. If it had tried to get out, it would have kept hitting the back of its head on the top rail of the fence. It probably figured it was safer—and less painful—just to stay put. Perhaps it had been trapped for several long hours. Would it have seemed long to a cow, I wondered? I decided to try and help. I had never been this close to a cow before, let alone touched one. I was a bit skittish. Nevertheless, I took the sides of its head in my hands and gently turned them to the side, until one ear was facing the sky. Amazingly, the cow stepped backwards, pulled its head out from between the fence rails, and then just lumbered off to rejoin the herd. A dog or cat in the same predicament would have been jumping out of their skin. But this huge, powerful animal was so calm and accepting of whatever came its way, whether hindrance or help. I feel that such a spirit deserves admiration and affection. I hope that cow is still there, munching sweet grass and happily hanging out with the rest of the herd.

Activity 39–2 (Editing I in Chapter 39 of *The Blair Handbook*)

39a Making pronouns agree with antecedents joined by and
39b Making pronouns agree with antecedents joined by or and nor
39c Making pronouns agree with collective nouns

Edit the following passage by making antecedents agree. Be especially careful about compound and collective antecedents.

Both the supervisor and her new assistant, James, are unhappy with his mutual arrangement. The supervisor admits that each regular task and special assignment is given the attention they deserve, but her assistant takes too much time to complete each one. The rest of the staff say it agrees with her. What does the assistant say in his own defense? As a junior person and a new member of the staff, he finds it difficult to handle new projects on their own and would like more help from his supervisor. He worries that someday either his irritation or his frustrations will make itself heard.

Activity 39–3 (Editing 2 in Chapter 39 of *The Blair Handbook*)

39 Making pronouns agree with indefinite pronouns

Edit the following passage by making pronouns and their indefinite pronoun antecedents agree. More than one edited version is possible.

Almost everyone knows that they can consult a thesaurus if they want to find a synonym for a given word. Some say that it is useful for improving his or her writing and public speaking. Many say that they use it to increase his or her vocabulary. A thesaurus can be a very good source for somebody who has a general idea in mind but needs a specific word or phrase. However, no one should rely too heavily on the thesaurus as a way for them to become a good writer. The best advice for someone is that they should concentrate on building a strong vocabulary first and consult a thesaurus second.

■ Activity 39–4

39e Making pronouns agree with antecedents that refer to amounts

Edit the following passage to make pronouns agree with their antecedents Be especially careful about antecedents that are amounts.

The ushers outside the movie house selected three-quarters of the audience and asked it to complete a form based on its responses to the film it was about to see. Ten percent threw its forms in the trash, but the remaining nine-tenths gave their various opinions on a number of subjects. Someone said that four hours feels like a long time when they aren't interrupted by an intermission. Considering that the film practically put them to sleep, a few complained of having to spend seven dollars. They thought that they could have been better spent on almost anything else. About half responded that it found the movie thrilling. Of that half, one hundred percent said it would recommend it to its friends.

Activity 39-5 (Editing 3 in Chapter 39 of *The Blair Handbook*)

Edit the following passage by making pronouns agree with their antecedents. (You may have to change some verbs and nouns as well.) More than one edited version is possible.

Changes in facial hair, a higher or lower voice, and a decreased sex drive: this is some of the side effects of taking steroids. Yet many continue in their use of this dangerous drug. Athletics is ever more competitive and athletes are always striving to be the best he or she can be. In a race, mere seconds are along time to an athlete when they mean the difference between a gold and silver medal. Perhaps the athlete does not know what harm they are doing to their bodies. There is no physical addiction to steroids; any addiction to it is psychological and based on the fact that athletes like what they see. Unfortunately, the athlete cannot always see what lies ahead for them. Ben Johnson and some others should count himself lucky. All Johnson lost was a gold medal and the chance to compete again. Benjamin Ramirez was not so lucky. Nor were the many like him who lost his life.

Clarifying Pronoun Reference

Edit the following passage to clarify pronoun reference. More than one edited version is possible.

A small but amazing revolution has recently taken place in New York City: the transformation of Bryant Park. Once it was a drug pushers' domain that law-abiding persons were careful to avoid. Now, after long and careful renovations, it is a safe, beautiful, welcoming spot that they eagerly seek out and linger in. If you have not been there, you must make a point to go with a companion and maybe a bag lunch. They let you have your choice of seating: benches under the trees alongside gravel walkways where you can watch people stroll or jog by; folding chairs that you can pick up and move anywhere your heart desires; or the broad, beautiful central lawn, where so many others are already lying in the sun. That is one of the best things about it. I myself love to take a chair and just rest in the sweet air and the calm atmosphere created by the trees, grass, and flowers. Birds are drawn to the park, too, and I love to watch them strut, peck, and swoop, which are endlessly interesting. To watch all the people is wonderful, too. Everyone is so relaxed. People, they are sitting alone on chairs, like I am, just looking around. They are not going anywhere. They are not fighting with each other over a cab. They are not cranky and nasty and cutthroat. Some of them, which are paired up, are lying on the grass, necking passionately or just napping peacefully. If you know the midtown area of New York City at all, you know how striking all this is. This park is a great gift to them.

Activity 40–2 (Editing I in Chapter 40 of *The Blair Handbook*)

40a Making each pronoun refer to a single antecedent

Edit the following passage by making each pronoun refer clearly to a single antecedent. More than one edited version is possible.

Diane spotted Laura as she was beginning her regimen of stretching exercises. It was twenty minutes before the race was due to begin. Diane told Laura that she thought she would win the race. She was just plain faster. Laura responded that she had a good chance, but that she was going to be tough to beat. Nodding in agreement, Diane shook hands with Laura. "Good luck," she said. "Have a good race."

Activity 40–3

40b Placing pronouns close to antecedents

Edit the following passage by placing pronouns close to there antecedents. More than one edited version is possible.

At the age of four, Wolfgang Amadeus Mozart impressed many of the courts throughout Europe by composing and playing music for the harpsichord, violin, and organ. That music was among the most beautiful ever heard or written, and it was obviously performed by a child prodigy, who later went on to write more than six hundred works in a very short time, including operas, symphonies, and many other instrumental works. Invited by the archbishop, he became concertmaster at Salzburg when he was still a teenager. When he was thirty-two years old, in a burst of creative activity Mozart composed three symphonies in three months.

■ Activity 40–4

40c Providing explicitly antecedents

Edit the following sentences to that all pronouns refer to explicit antecedents. Make any small changes in wording that are needed for clarity. More than one edited version is possible.

1. Animal rights groups are pleased that a new ruling will guarantee more of them to animals in labs nationwide.

2. Some lab assistants were charged with treating the animals badly, which animal rights groups took very seriously.

3. Animal rights organizations pay attention to the research in labs, and they publish studies about abuses of them.

4. Researchers who do not meet the new standards will have to pay high fines, which might make them more willing to cooperate.

5. Scientists said the new law would prevent them from performing experiments that might benefit humans. This is not surprising.

6. Animal rights groups were charged with wanting to treat them like humans.

7. Not walking the dogs showed lack of concern for their welfare.

8. The animals' cages were dirty and uncomfortable for them.

9. The director of one research center said that the implications for labs would be grave. This is true.

10. The ruling also affects primates, which are used in psychological and behavioral experiments.

Activity 40–5 (Editing 2 in Chapter 40 of *The Blair Handbook*)

40c Providing explicit antecedents

Edit the following passage by making all pronouns refer to explicit antecedents. More than one edited version is possible.

The fraternity house that I visited was not as neat inside as I had expected from knowing them. Its old and worn furniture may have made it look worse than it was, but I for one didn't feel like sitting down on any of the couches. The fraternity brothers made it sound like the best thing in the world to be a part of. Downstairs there was a huge crowd. The brothers said that most nights a long line to get food stretches out into the hall, with everybody pushing to get to the front. This is typical. The brothers wall pretty nice, but at one point in the evening they had a toast to the crowd and they threw garbage on everyone at the party, which I didn't think was too nice.

Activity 40–6 (Editing 3 in Chapter 40 of *The Blair Handbook*)

40d Replacing a vague <u>it</u>, <u>they</u>, or <u>you</u>
40e Avoiding overuse of <u>it</u>

Edit the following passage by clarifying all uses of the pronouns *it*, *they*, and *you*. Make any small changes in wording that are needed for smooth reading. More than one edited version is possible.

They say that you shouldn't believe everything you read in the newspaper. It is foolish to assume that it is possible for it to be accurate all of the time. You can't expect that there will never be a mistake. Sometimes they get late-breaking stories and have to rush to get them in before it goes to press. Occasionally you can even see contradictions between two articles on the same topic. It will say one thing in one article and then it will say something different in the other. It is when that happens that it is hard for you to know which article you should believe.

■ **Activity 40–7** (Editing 4 in Chapter 40 of *The Blair Handbook*)

40f Choosing <u>who</u>, <u>which</u>, or <u>that</u> according to the antecedent

Complete the following passage, filling in the blanks with the correct pronoun: *who, which,* or *that.*

None of the carpenters _____ I know has any use for imported nails. They swear that American-made nails are the only ones _____ are worth using. A nail _____ bends when it is driven in was probably made in Canada, they say. One box of nails, _____ they got from Japan, had heads _____ broke off if they tried to pull them out. There are problems every time the contractor brings them boxes _____ are imported. These carpenters, every one of _____ works with nails every day, believe that they can tell where a nail comes from as soon as they hit it with a hammer. One thing is certain: a bent nail doesn't get that way because a carpenter hit it crooked.

■ **Activity 40–8** (Editing 5 in Chapter 40 of *The Blair Handbook*)

Edit the following passage by making sure that all pronoun references are clear and that all pronouns are used appropriately. More than one edited version is possible.

Studies have shown that alcoholism is a major problem in our city, which has a high percentage of unemployed and homeless people. This is true in other metropolitan areas as well. However, it affects not only the down-and-out but also working people, the elderly, and teenagers which have begun to experiment with drinking. We interviewed some social workers, which said that being homeless caused some people to drink. What we learned from interviewing homeless people, though, was that many of those which are homeless now, they were drinking long before they were on the street. Drink hard enough and long enough and you inevitably lose your home, it seems from their experience.

Choosing the Correct Pronoun Case

Activity 41-1

Edit the following passage to make sure all pronouns are in the correct case. More than one edited version is possible.

The art world is full of stories of intrigue and deception. For example in 1938 three men were hired to restore some thirteenth-century cathedral wall paintings in Schleswig, Germany. Fey, Fey, and Malskat began by cleaning all the paintings. But underneath the work of a previous restorer named Ohlbers, there was practically nothing left of the paintings theirselves! The three men must have thought them to have only one option. They simply produced brand-new paintings, based on their memory of the ones they had removed during the cleaning process. These "restorations" were enchanting to whoever they were shown. Viewing they revealed surprising details about history. For instance, there were a lot of turkeys in these "restored" paintings. Scholars had believed that Europe's first turkeys were brought over from America in the sixteenth century. Now it seemed there were actually turkeys in Germany three hundred years before Columbus had even landed in America! Perhaps there had been trade between the two worlds at that early date. But this seemed unlikely. Finally, Ohlbers made a statement to this effect: In my day, us restorers would always add something of our own anywhere in a painting that was blank or impossible to make out. He had, very innocently, painted a couple of turkeys. Fey, Fey, and Malskat had just added many more. Ohlbers and them had simply made a chain of honest mistakes. Twenty years and many acclaimed "restorations" later the full truth came out. Malskat was in fact a talented forger, and the Feys were his partners in crime. Whom blew the whistle? Malskat hisself did, because of an unsettled score between he and the Feys. The Feys had gotten fare more glory, credit, and pay for their work than him. Malskat wanted his own fair share. What he got was a prison sentence.

■ **Activity 41-2** (Editing 1 in Chapter 41 of *The Blair Handbook*)

41a Choosing case for compound elements

Edit the following sentences, using the appropriate pronoun case for compound subjects and objects.

1. To him and I they provide hours of entertainment and neither he nor me ever seems to tire of them.

2. I don't remember if it was him or me who first started watching them.

3. Others may not appreciate our passion for these shows, but they never seem boring to either he or I.

4. The best ones make me and him laugh every time we see them, and, thanks to the invention of the VCR, him and I can see them over and over.

5. Me and him have seen some shows so many times that we have practically memorized them.

■ Activity 41–3

41b Choosing case for appositive pronouns

Edit the following sentences, using the appropriate case for appositive pronouns.

1. All three hikers—him, her and me—had expected the colored marks on the trees to lead us back to the head of the trail.

2. Fallen trees along the path prevented even the most determined hikers—Sarah and I— from following the trail.

3. The optimists among us, Christopher and me, knew we would eventually find our way out of the woods.

4. When the ordeal was over, the more experienced members told the three thankful hikers—Christopher, Sarah, and I—that they had been worried about us.

5. The most enthusiastic members of the expedition, Sarah and me, were ready to go back into the woods the next day.

Activity 41–4

41c Choosing between <u>us</u> and <u>we</u> before a noun

Edit the following sentences, using *us* and *we* correctly.

1. Us reporters took notes on the relief plan as the president spoke.

2. Officials who spoke off the record gave we media people the impression that the operation would not last long.

3. They told we members of the press that the president wanted to improve conditions for the suffering people.

4. Us feature writers plan to concentrate on the humanitarian efforts of the administration.

5. The president told we newswriters that he hoped that other countries would also participate.

Activity 41–5 (Editing 2 in Chapter 41 of *The Blair Handbook*)

41a Choosing case for compound elements

41b Choosing case for appositive pronouns

41c Choosing between <u>us</u> and <u>we</u> before a noun

Edit the following paragraph, using the appropriate pronoun cases. Watch out for pronouns in compound subjects and objects, pronouns used as appositives, and *us* and *we* before nouns.

Fishing with our dad, Charley and me hadn't caught any fish all week. We decided it was up to the two of us, him and I, to find some way to catch something. Us two kids borrowed a rowboat and, with him and me rowing, went way out in the middle of the pond. We dropped anchor and began fishing, him out of one side of the boat and I out of the other side. Charley asked me if I was sleepy and I said, "Not me," but then a splash of water woke me, and the boat was rocking. Charley was pulling madly on his rod, and it seemed as if his catch would tip the boat over and he and I with it. It took ten minutes for us, Charley and I, to get that catfish on board. Dad said it was turning out that the real fishers in the family were Charley and me. Dad made both Charley and I feel really proud.

Activity 41–6

41d Choosing case with verbals

Edit the following sentences, using the correct pronoun case with verbals. Some sentences have more than one possible answer.

1. George looked positively stunned by us yelling "Surprise!" when he opened the door.

2. It was amusing for we to watch his unwrapping the gifts that we brought.

3. As we waited for George to cut the cake, it seemed to us that him thanking everyone for

    the gifts was taking forever.

4. We all sang "Happy Birthday" and watched his blowing out the candles.

5. The occasion called for him eating the biggest piece of cake.

Activity 41–7 (Editing 3 in Chapter 41 of *The Blair Handbook*)

41e Choosing case after <u>than</u> or <u>as</u>

Edit the following sentences, using the correct pronoun case after *than* and *as*. Circle the number of any sentence that is correct.

1. I consider myself just as good an announcer had her.

2. Me playing the latest hits has contributed to my success.

3. Surveys show that her programs appeal to a wider audience than me.

4. The other station in town would like we to be less popular.

5. We give out more free tickets to performances than them.

6. One thing is for sure: we don't play as much dull music as they.

■ Activity 41–8 (Editing 4 in Chapter 41 of *The Blair Handbook*)

41f Choosing between <u>who</u> and <u>whom</u>

Edit the following passage, using *who, whom, whoever,* and *whomever* correctly.

Whomever was it who said that the shortest distance between two points is a straight line? I don't know, but it was certainly someone wise. This maxim implies directness, and anybody whom is trying to write effectively should keep these words in mind. Karen Branch, who is featured regularly in my favorite magazine, knows how to be direct and get to the point. Right at the start, Branch makes the content of an article perfectly clear to whomever is reading it. By avoiding rambling musings and cute anecdotes she gives to the reader who she is addressing only the facts—the what, where, when, how, and whom. Everyone who reads her articles, whomever they are, admires her for her integrity.

■ Activity 41–9

41g Using reflexive pronouns as objects

Edit the following sentences, using the correct reflexive pronoun. Circle the number of any sentence that is correct.

1. My friend Mark tells stories as much to amuse him as the rest of us.

2. According to my friends and myself, there's no better place to swap stories than the neighborhood coffeehouse.

3. My friends and myself often laugh among ourselves when we recall our favorite tales from high school.

4. Sometimes when we get going, we tell ourselves not to be so noisy, and sometimes the coffeehouse owner tells us the same.

5. If you were to ask my friends and myself what word best describes ourselves, we would say "comrades."

Activity 41–10 (Editing 5 in Chapter 41 of *The Blair Handbook*)

Edit the following passage, using the appropriate pronoun cases throughout.

In the memories of my siblings and myself, our house used to be surrounded by a forest on three sides. Us children—my three brothers and me—used to hunt for snakes and salamanders in the woods by overturning the rocks that they lived under. One of the best hunting rounds for ourselves was the land to the south of our yard. When I was eight years old, I saw a garter snake catch a frog and devour it whole. It eating the frog upset my brothers and I terribly. Us, with our childish minds, thought that snakes were nasty, cruel creatures and that frogs were clearly nicer than them. Now that I am grown up, I realize that the snake eating the frog was not an act of cruelty. Snakes eat frogs to survive just as frogs eat insects. Each creature on earth lives and dies according to the natural order of things.

■ Activity 41-11

Edit the following passage, using correct pronoun cases.

John, who we all thought of as an outstanding student, was almost expelled last semester. His friend Dave and him were considered the two strongest scholars in the department. Whatever intellectual debate us all engaged in—whether inside the classroom or out—those two always seemed to win the argument. Then John started spending less time on his studies and more time with a group of people who he referred to only as "The Brothers."

John once said, "Us students have to hit the books week after week if we really want to excel. You're only as good as your last paper." But now he spent all his time with his new friends, and none of us challenged him wasting his days with them. Whomever knew about it just kept quiet. As for myself, I never asked him why I saw him at the library so infrequently. I guess we all figured it was something he would work out for himself. None of us were happy with him failing class after class. But by the end of the semester, the damage was done.

Making Sentences Consistent and Complete

Edit the following passage to make all sentences consistent and complete. More than one edited version is possible.

We tend to think of technological change and the dangers it poses as problems unique to our time. But there has always been technological growth of some kind, and always that growth will bring unexpected pitfalls. Can we imagine, for instance, that the Pyramids, the great Gothic cathedrals, the Roman viaducts, and the Great Wall of China were built without unfortunate incidents or injuries to the workers? In early America, improvements in home heating apparatuses, new building techniques and materials, and closer placement of houses as towns grew larger and larger. All these things led to frequent unmanageable fires now would start and spread more easily. In time, the coping mechanism of fire houses and trained fire fighters were devised and implemented. Later on, steamboat travel was all the rage. But the steam engines were prone to explosions. In one five-year period, 270 deaths resulted in such explosions. The government finally stepped in to insisted on safer designs. Train travel brought newly hazardous. At one point, twenty-five railroad bridges were collapsing every year. What is comforting is where society has found safeguards against so many of these life-threatening perils. We have learned from centuries of mistakes; maybe humanity will eventually learn to anticipate the threats our progress can pose.

Activity 42-2 (Editing 2 in Chapter 42 of *The Blair Handbook*)

42a Avoiding unnecessary shifts

Edit the following sentences to avoid distracting or awkward shifts. Some sentences have more than one possible answer.

1. The entire freshman class did well on their exam.

2. We were given one hour for the examination, and do not use any books.

3. We were told first to review the instructions, and then you can begin to answer the questions.

4. The professor said, "The examination will conclude in one hour", and that we had to answer all of the questions in two out of three sections.

5. After the exam was over, the professor tells us it counts for half of the final grade.

6. When a student completes the exam and puts down their pen, they often feel a great sense of relief that it is over.

7. One student works through the questions too quickly and many mistakes are made.

8. The marking of the exams is up to the teaching assistant, but they don't usually assign the final grade.

Activity 42–3

42a Avoiding unnecessary shifts

Edit the following passage to avoid distracting shifts. More than one edited version is possible.

Recently the Abenaki tribe petitioned the state for tribal recognition. In such cases the court looks for documented political continuity. The Abenaki don't operate under a formal hierarchical political system, but instead they are governed by the general will of their members. Consequently, they have few written records documenting their government. After the presentation was made before the court, the state reviews the case and denied the Abenaki recognition. The tribe's spokesperson said, "The claimed we didn't fulfill the burden of proof" and that the state denied them recognition.

◼ Activity 42–4

42b Eliminating mixed constructions

Edit the following sentences by eliminating mixed constructions. Some sentences have more than one possible answer.

1. The outrageous exploitation of our natural resources has diminished to the point where several species are threatened or endangered.

2. The fact that spotted owls has transmitters placed on them measured their range.

3. The calculations of the study counted the owls with transmitters to learn how much territory they would need.

4. When a forest is preserved in parcels of five square miles strictly curtails the logging there.

5. The situation with extensive clear-cutting of the old-growth forest has destroyed the owl's natural habitat.

6. An old-growth forest is when trees of various ages, up to several hundred years old, and several species live together in an undisturbed way.

7. The reason old-growth forests are important is because many creatures live there that cannot survive on tree farms.

8. A tree farm is when the ancient forest is cut down and whole areas of new trees are planted.

Activity 42–5 (Editing 3 in Chapter 42 of *The Blair Handbook*)

42b Eliminating mixed constructions

Edit the following passage by eliminating mixed constructions. More than one edited version is possible.

The dissatisfaction of community members often charges that important decisions are made behind closed doors, or at least doors without welcome signs. The reason is because many feel it is their right to have information ahead of time about the decisions made at town meetings. Local newspapers usually have summaries of town affairs, but some say they are never totally accurate or very thorough. By feeling that they don't have to check with members of the community before voting on every issue means the local officials are confident of their own opinions. Being an elected official is when you make certain decisions on behalf of the members of the community.

■ **Activity 42–6** (Editing 4 in Chapter 42 of *The Blair Handbook*)

42c Finishing incomplete sentences

Edit the following passage adding any necessary words to elliptical structures, making all comparisons complete by adding all necessary words that may have been inadvertently omitted. More than one edited version is possible.

It's important to keep in mind that the children at the community center are individuals. No child's problems are the same as another. Change is difficult for everyone, children more so. Some of the children here are severely emotionally disturbed. The goal of the center is assess each child's needs to discover those who need a lot of attention and those who need less attention. For youths who are severely emotionally disturbed, their disturbance is an invisible handicap and becomes more apparent at stressful times. The behavior ranges of emotionally disturbed children are wider than adults. The social workers give the children's lives a sense of structure, the schedule stability.

■ **Activity 42–7** (Editing 5 in Chapter 42 of *The Blair Handbook*)

Edit the following passage, making all sentences consistent and complete. More than one edited version is possible.

I'll bet that most people sit down to their dinner between six and seven o'clock each night. You can tell because that's when the infuriating salespeople from the local paper call. He pretends that I already have a subscription, and then he'll ask you. "Was your paper delivered on time today?" or whether it was late. It is especially annoying is where they ask the same question every time. And they think that if you say, "No, I'm not a subscriber," somehow I will agree to listen to their sales pitch. What makes it even worse is a terrible newspaper. If they were trying to sell me the *New York Times* would be different story.

End Punctuation

Edit the following passage, making sure that periods, exclamation points, and question marks are used correctly.

Many people have asked me what it takes to be a successful triathlon competitor? Incredible physical stamina. An obsessive personality. A bit of both? I guess it does take a particular personality. Let's face it: sweating and straining for more than an hour isn't everyone's idea of a good time, is it. My last triathlon, for example, was probably the most difficult I have ever completed. It started out well enough. In fact, I couldn't believe how easy the 3/4-kilometer swim was for me. The next phase of the race was the 20-kilometer bicycle race. Was that ever hard? The Santa Fe course is challenging at the best of times, but on that day, a drizzle had begun falling at around 6:00 A.M. By the time the race began, the road surface was dangerously slick. In a race in the Southwest, I never expected—who would—to encounter such treacherous conditions for biking. Wouldn't you know that the one day it would rain in months would be the day of our race? The ride went better than I had expected, considering I had to ride more slowly than usual. And am I glad I did? Right in front of me, the Michigan woman's back wheel slid out from under her. Talk about a nerve-wracking ride. By the time I started the 5-kilometer road race at the end, I was so tense that I couldn't find a good stride. I never did make up the lost time, and, even though my finishing time was under two hours—can you believe it!—I felt terrible at the end. But I never let a bad race make me discouraged. There's always another race, isn't there.

Activity 43-2 (Editing 1 in Chapter 43 of *The Blair Handbook*)

43a Using periods at the ends of sentences

43b Using periods with abbreviations

43c Using question marks

Edit the following sentences by using periods correctly.

1. Because he is so interested in the 5th century B.C., Carlos usually does well on ancient history tests.

2. He especially likes the period ca 455-430 B.C., when Athenian culture was at its height.

3. The note on the board reads: "For tomorrow's test, please read Chapter 7 (pp 100-133)."

4. Rob asks if he can borrow Carlos's notes to study for the test?

5. Rob sometimes wonders how much studying will be enough?

Activity 43-3 (Editing 2 in Chapter 43 of *The Blair Handbook*)

43c Using question marks

Edit the following sentences by using question marks correctly.

1. I wonder how long it takes to be able to think in a different language?

2. What is the best way for me to learn to speak French. Converse with my friends. Go to the language lab. Go to France?

3. The best way to learn to speak another language is to speak it as often as possible, isn't it.

4. Some students think it's entertaining (?) when classmates make mistakes.

5. You know, don't you, that we learn by making mistakes.

■ **Activity 43-4** (Editing 4 in Chapter 43 in *The Blair Handbook*)

43d Using exclamation points

Edit the following sentences by using exclamation points correctly. Some sentences have more than one possible answer.

1. "Be careful," she called out as we hurried down the icy driveway.

2. "Oh! No! Here comes the bus now. Hurry up."

3. "Too late. Now we'll have to walk to school."

4. "Are you crazy? It's a four-mile walk to school."

5. "Don't tell me you can't walk four miles?" I exclaimed.

■ **Activity 43-5** (Editing 5 in Chapter 43 in *The Blair Handbook*)

43   End punctuation

Edit the following passage by using all end punctuation correctly. More than one edited version is possible.

What a morning. I wonder if you ever had the kind of morning when everything seems to go wrong? First I overslept (!) because my alarm clock didn't go off Then I was hurrying to make my class and I tripped and fell and skinned my knee. I rushed into the classroom and saw my classmates clearing off their desks and taking out clean sheets of paper? I asked someone whether we were having a test? She whispered back, "Don't you remember. It's our Roman history test. On the collapse of the empire!" Of course. How could I have forgotten. "When was that," I whispered. "It was 133-31 B.C.," she whispered back. Then Professor Martin wanted to know why I wasn't sitting down? Was I planning to join the rest of the class today. "What else can I do now?," I muttered under my breath as I took my seat. "All right, everybody," he said. "On your mark. Get set. Go. Start writing."

■ ■ ■
Commas

Edit the following passage, making sure that commas are used where required.

Many Americans wonder if the day will ever come, when we elect a woman to the office of the president. Why is it that the United States which considers itself a leader among nations, lags so far behind many other, developed nations in this area? The names of many past and present women leaders of other countries spring easily to mind including Gandhi Thatcher Bhutto and Meir. And in 1993 two, more women added their names to the list: Tansu Ciller prime minister of Turkey and Kim Campbell prime minister of Canada. Without question there are qualified women for the position so why can't a women get elected? What is it about Americans, which makes us unwilling to take this step? To find out why it is instructive to examine how those nations run by women differ from the United States. Take Canada for example whose society and lifestyle most people assume is similar to our own. But, is it? Not in this area it isn't. A few examples will illustrate how far ahead of us Canadians are in their attitudes toward feminist issues. In Canada women's rights organizations receive funding from the federal government to keep them thriving; Canada's ERA has been a part of its constitution for more than ten years; and women's studies programs are offered in every major university. Furthermore Canada stands far ahead of the United States in the areas of equal pay for women and maternity leave not to mention the number of women in the government at all levels. Clearly we as Americans are going to have to change our attitudes toward women in general before we ever see a woman in the White House.

Activity 44-2 (Editing 1 in Chapter 44 of *The Blair Handbook*)

44a Using commas before coordinating conjunctions joining independent clauses

Edit the following sentences with coordinating conjunctions joining independent clauses, using commas correctly. Circle the number of any sentence that is correct.

1. Every new business or residence along a highway needs an access road but first the highway department must approve its design and location.

2. The developer of a new housing development or commercial center must complete an application, and must submit it for the highway department's review.

3. The standards for sight distances and markings are very clearly described in the regulations so a developer can tell if a driveway is acceptable.

4. The minimum sight distances vary with the speed limit and the grade of the road and the standards for driveway construction vary with the expected volume of traffic.

5. The highway department does not have to permit a driveway that does not meet its standards or that would require modifications to the roadway.

Activity 44-3

44a Using commas before coordinating conjunctions joining independent clauses

Edit the following sentences by using a comma and a coordinating conjunction to join two sentences into one sentence. Most sentences can be edited in more than one way.

1. The developer wants a commercial driveway for a new business along Highway 225. The highway department may have several objections.

2. The road at that point is very steep. Traffic moves very fast.

3. The driveway would be close to a curve. It would be hard to see.

4. Traffic coming down the hill would have to slow down behind anyone turning into the driveway. The driveway is so close to the curve that there could be an accident.

5. The driveway would be obscured by trees and shrubs. Drivers would not be able to see it.

Activity 44-4

44a Using commas before coordinating conjunctions joining independent clauses

44b Using commas after introductory elements

Edit the following passage, making sure that commas are used correctly with introductory elements and with coordinating conjunctions in compound sentences.

Originally called the "Women's Liberation Movement" the women's movement as we know it was founded during the 1960s. Although the impact of the modern women's movement should not be underestimated the campaign for greater rights for women did not begin at that decade. More than a century earlier the first women's rights convention convened in the New York town of Seneca Falls and its main purpose was to address the issue of a woman's right to vote. Elizabeth Cady Stanton and Lucretia Mott were both prominent abolitionists in the 1840s and they also campaigned hard for women's rights. The nineteenth-century movement succeeded in convincing thousands of men and women that women should have the vote but women's suffrage did not become a reality until 1920, with the 19th Amendment.

■ **Activity 44-5** (Editing 2 in Chapter 44 of *The Blair Handbook*)

44b Using commas after introductory elements

Edit the following passage, using commas after introductory elements.

When she met Alfred Stieglitz Georgia O'Keeffe was studying at the Art Students League. Then twenty years old O'Keeffe visited Stieglitz's famous 291 gallery and became acquainted with the pioneering photographer. About eight years later she sent some drawings to a friend, and the friend showed them to Stieglitz. Without asking her permission he hung them in his gallery. She demanded that he take them down, but he did not. Nearly a year later he mounted a solo exhibit of her work, and their alliance was fully established.

■ **Activity 44-6** (Editing 3 in Chapter 44 of *The Blair Handbook*)

44c Using commas to set off nonrestrictive modifiers and appositives

Edit the following passage, using commas with nonrestrictive modifiers and appositives.

A personal computer that essential tool of college work is not just a necessity but a requirement on many campuses. Many schools that once did not require computers have changed their policies. Even these schools the late entries into the personal computer age have mainframe computers for business or scientific applications but usually these are not readily available to large numbers of undergraduate students. The move to computers is happening nearly equally in engineering and humanities departments both of which can put computers to good use although they use them in entirely different ways. In requiring students to own personal computers colleges have had to specify the kind of computer students should use. Colleges then have had to teach students how to use them which has not always been easy.

Activity 44-7

44c Using commas to set off nonrestrictive modifiers and appositives

Edit the following passage, making sure that commas are used correctly with restrictive and nonrestrictive modifiers and appositives. More than one edited version is possible.

No one, who has been to the top of Mount Battie on the coast of Maine, can fail to be struck by the scenic beauty of the landscape, which is visible for miles. It is easy to appreciate the feelings, which inspired American poet, Edna St. Vincent Millay, to write her famous poem, "Renascence." At the top of the mountain near a bronze plaque that commemorates the veterans, who fought in World War I, is a plaque, explaining that Millay wrote her poem while enjoying the view from the summit. The magnificent view, which inspired her, is virtually unchanged today, and thousands of visitors go to Mount Battie every year to enjoy the same sweeping views of the mountains and the sea.

■ Activity 44-8

44c Using commas to set off nonrestrictive modifiers and appositives

Edit the following sentences to make sure that commas are used correctly with modifiers and appositives. Circle the number of any sentence that is correct.

1. The workers in the pasteurization room who are all dressed alike wear white uniforms, blue hats, black boots, and belts.

2. Manager Karen Owens explained that the cows that she keeps include Holsteins, Jerseys, and Guernseys.

3. The farm's pasteurizer whose pipes carry milk back and forth and through a coil heats milk for fifteen minutes and then quickly cools it.

4. Of the two homogenizers, the machine, on the left, has pistons at the front, designed to force the milk though small valves.

5. In the last part of the system which is the packaging machine heat lamps melt wax, and the containers get shaped and sealed.

Activity 44-9 (Editing 4 in Chapter 44 of *The Blair Handbook*)

44d Using commas between elements in a series and between coordinate adjectives

Edit the following sentences, using commas correctly between items in a series and between coordinate adjectives. Circle the number of any sentence that is correct.

1. Inside the airport are a comfortable lounge, three departure gates, and a restaurant.

2. The airport leases the space to a number of customers, including airlines car rental agencies food concessions and gift shops.

3. The airport's representative explained that the airport is run like larger airports that it leases out its buildings and that it takes a percentage of the profits made by the independent businesses.

4. The majority of air travel at the airport is between Boston Newark and Chicago, although travel is by no means limited to these three, major cities.

5. Over the next ten years, the airport hopes to replace the few, remaining pre-1950s buildings with large modern facilities.

Activity 44-10 (Editing 5 in Chapter 44 of *The Blair Handbook*)

44e Using commas to set off parenthetical elements

Edit the following sentences, using commas correctly with parenthetical expressions. Circle the number of any sentence that is correct.

1. "Is today in fact the day the papers are due?" I have heard that question more often than I choose to remember let me tell you.

2. Since weekly papers are due every Monday, it should come as no surprise although it often does when Monday rolls around with such relentless regularity.

3. Just this morning, for example, some students asked me whether I might allow them to turn in Monday's paper on Tuesday.

4. "Certainly," I replied. I added however that today's essay submitted tomorrow should be worth at least as much as yesterday's newspaper delivered today.

5. "However, there is you should know one important difference between a newspaper company and me. A newspaper company on the one hand gives credit for a paper that is one day late, while I on the other hand do not."

Activity 44-11 (Editing 6 in Chapter 44 of *The Blair Handbook*)

44f Using commas to set off elements of contrast, tag sentences, and words of direct address

Edit the following sentences, using commas correctly to set off elements of contrast, tag questions, and words of direct address. Circle the number of any sentence that is correct.

1. Most people over seventy-five own their homes my friends not because they have a lot of money but because they purchased them years ago, when housing prices were low.

2. Often elderly people who want to be independent have to live in conditions they consider less than ideal don't they?

3. The children of the elderly, not the elderly themselves, tend to worry about illness and accidents.

4. The growing numbers of people over age eighty-five are in better not worse condition than their predecessors.

5. Given that they are in better condition, many are able if not eager to live alone.

Activity 44-12 (Editing 7 in Chapter 44 of *The Blair Handbook*)

44g Using commas with quotations

Edit the following sentences, using commas correctly with quotations.

1. "I don't know" Danielle replied "but I think that Terry has a good chance"

2. "Did Dolores say anything about the current," Danielle inquired? "Where is it strongest?"

3. Isabella replied "The current is strongest in the deepest part of the channel, but the seaweed in the shallow parts can really slow the boat down."

4. As the gun went off, Isabella muttered "If we lose this race, then all the time and effort that we spent will be for nothing!"

■ **Activity 44-13** (Editing 8 in Chapter 44 of *The Blair Handbook*)

44h Using commas with numbers, dates, names, and addresses

Edit the following sentences, using commas correctly with numbers, dates, names, and addresses.

1. I started my job in February, 1993, and the last day I worked was January 15 1994.

2. During that time, I answered 3456 calls and sold merchandise worth more than $200000.

3. The worst customers are the ones with names like Jane Jones Ph.D. or John Johnson, III, who insist on having their titles appear on all their mail.

4. You may write to my former employer at this address: National Mail-Order Products, 19123 Fifth Avenue New York New York 10001.

5. With $1500 in my savings account, I do not need to worry about getting another job until March 1994.

■ **Activity 44-14**

44i Using commas to prevent misreading

Edit the following sentences, inserting commas wherever necessary to prevent misreading

1. What the defendant's alibi is simply incredible.

2. Before the defendant was involved in similar crimes.

3. They are to listen to the prosecutor and defense lawyer and judge the defendant as they deem fit.

4. The verdict came in record time.

5. In keeping with what is permitted by the law firm punishment is expected.

Activity 44-15 (Editing 11 in Chapter 44 of *The Blair Handbook*)

44j   Avoiding the misuse of commas

Edit the following passage by deleting any unnecessary commas.

All of the students who live in the co-op on campus, work together, to keep the place clean. It usually takes about half an hour to clean the dorm, and each person cleans twice a month. The job of the "whip" is, to make sure the cleaning is done. If the job has not been done, when the whip checks it, the student, who is responsible, is given a demerit point. Students must accumulate fewer than three demerit points, or be forced to move out of the co-op. If the whip says that, a job has been done poorly,the student has to do it again. Cleaning up after others, is not a lot of fun, but I have to admit that, the co-op is the cleanest dorm on campus.

Activity 44-16

44j   Avoiding the misuse of commas

Edit the following sentences, deleting any unnecessary commas. Circle the number of any sentence that is correct.

1. What made this year special, was that, I was entering college.

2. I had to confess that, the thought of being in a school with thousands of students,

    made me nervous.

3. A bit unsure of what to expect, but also excited, I got out of bed.

4. What seemed to fear most, was that I would make embarrassing mistakes, and

    humiliate myself in front of thousands of strangers.

5. Not surprisingly a number of things did go wrong, but I told myself that life could only

    get better.

Activity 44-17 (Editing 12 in Chapter 44 of *The Blair Handbook*)

Edit the following passage, using commas correctly.

In recent years growing numbers of distinguished, economics experts have presented a disturbing if not totally grim financial forecast for the United States and the world. In fact some predict a total, global, economic collapse before December 31 1999. Anyone, who listens to their dire predictions might wonder if they are just trying to sell their wares or if there is some validity to their forecasts. A number of sources point out, that there are increasing numbers of financial failures which they say are the first sign of the impending collapse. Banks provide the mechanism for the flow of money and money flow is very complicated. There are two, main resources, where banks get their money for credit, the Federal Reserve System, and their depositors' savings accounts. They prefer the latter which requires them to pay less interest. In these supposedly dire economic times many banks are becoming involved in mergers, a development that economic forecasters see as another sign of collapse.

Semicolons

Edit the following passage, using semicolons where they are correct and effective.

That summer the river rose higher than anyone thought possible. No one alive had ever seen anything like it, in fact, it had never been so high—not since the county started keeping records. Every morning when we woke up, we would go to the windows; hoping to make out even one ray of sunlight slanting through the clouds. But day after day after day we saw only gray—gray clouds, gray rain, gray skies. The sun was nowhere to be seen. We tuned in to the radio constantly. It was our only link with the outside world. The station broadcast around the clock, keeping us up-to-date on every aspect of the flood; the latest relief efforts, where volunteers were needed next, and, of course, the latest weather forecast. We river people are stubborn, I guess. For a long time, nobody was willing to leave. We had all seen heavy rains before, and we had always come out all right. So we stayed on; hoping that today might bring the change we were looking for. By the ninth day, the town's fresh water supply ran out. Most people finally gave up and evacuated. But some people still refused to go; even though staying now meant they risked losing more than their homes. They had lived there all their lives, life anywhere else was simply unimaginable. It took about a month; but the river did eventually subside. How we got rid of the mud is another story.

Activity 45-2 (Editing 2 in Chapter 45 of *The Blair Handbook*)

45a Using semicolons between independent clauses

Edit the following sentences, using semicolons as necessary to join independent clauses.

1. The center provides a very structured environment for the children, for example, there are rules to follow and expectations to meet.

2. For some emotionally disturbed children, school is a very difficult place, with its emphasis on adaptability, attentiveness, and obedience, yet the structure of a school environment benefits the children greatly.

3. When children act inappropriately, teachers try to reassure them that they still care for them, but children have to take responsibility for their actions.

4. Their ultimate goal is to prepare students for successful reintegration into the educational mainstream, consequently, they teach the academic and social skills necessary to be successful at school.

5. The teachers develop a suitable program for each child, discuss the program with the child's parents, and, with their approval, implement the program, but the child is the one who determines the success of the program.

Activity 45-3

45a using semicolons between independent clauses

Edit the following pairs of sentences, using a semicolon to join them. Add conjunctive adverbs, transitional expressions, or coordinating conjunctions if appropriate to express the relationships between the sentences. Some sentences can be edited in more than one way.

1. The shelter gives the homeless free food, does not impose a limit to the number of

    nights they can stay, and does not require guests to do any work around the place.

    Many of the young people treat it like one big party.

2. The shelter's intentions are only the best. The results are less than desirable.

3. The manager of the Salvation Army shelter, who is an ordained minister, runs the thrift

    store, oversees the soup kitchen, performs church services, and supervises fundraising

    efforts. He still finds time to visit with the residents every night.

4. Many homeless people tend either to go someplace warmer in the winter or to find more

    permanent living arrangements. Attendance at area shelters actually goes down.

5. Many people who use the East Side shelter are either working or have found a place to

    live within six weeks of leaving the shelter. That emergency shelter's success rate is 80

    percent.

Activity 45-4

45a Using semicolons between independent clauses

Edit the following passage, using semicolons between independent clauses wherever you think they are effective. More that one edited version is possible.

At the beginning, many people referred to it as the "growth bill," for its point was to help towns regain some control over the growing development that threatened their way of life. For the bill to succeed, participation among town residents was strongly encouraged. In fact, citizen participation was key. Some of the citizens, who had a bad relationships with local officials, were skeptical. Others were willing to give it a try. In the case of one supporter, repeated examples of poor planning and improper zoning eventually go to him, and, finally, he just had to get involved.

Activity 45-5 (Editing 3 in Chapter 45 of *The Blair Handbook*)

45b Using semicolons in complex series

Edit the following sentences, using semicolons as necessary in complex series.

1. Several different craft can be seen on the Charles Rivers, including sculls rowed by students from the universities in the area, canoes, rowboats, which can be rented for a small fee, and motorboats.

2. To get to know a new place quickly, obtain a detailed map of the area you plan to visit, walk to as many places as possible, always wearing shoes with good soles, and talk to the residents, provided they look friendly.

3. If you go to Boston's Museum of Fine Arts, don't miss the Paul Revere silver, the Egyptian mummies, the Athenian vases, and the terrific collection of paintings, including works by Gauguin, Degas, Monet, van Gogh, and Whistler.

4. If you really want to fit in, ask someone where the locals eat, find out how to get there, using public transportation, of course, and get to your destination without even consulting your subway map.

5. New England has produced some of the greatest writers in America: Henry David Thoreau, who wrote, *Walden,* Henry Wadsworth Longfellow, whose house on Brattle Street in Cambridge is a historic landmark, and Nathaniel Hawthorne, a resident of Salem, Massachusetts, and author of *The Scarlet Letter.*

Activity 45-6 (Editing 4 in Chapter 45 of *The Blair Handbook*)

45c Avoiding misuses of semicolons

Edit the following sentences by placing any incorrectly used semicolons with the correct mark of punctuation or rewording the sentence. Some sentences can be edited in more than one way. Circle the number of any sentence that is correct.

1. His writing abounds with examples of the greedy nature of human beings; however, it does not convey a sense of helplessness.

2. Mowat clings to a spark of hope that it is not too late for humans to develop a respectful attitude toward our planet and the animals that inhabit it; although he regards humans as covetous.

3. A self-designated advocate for nonhuman animals, Mowat reveals the precariousness of the relationship between humans and animals; with unforgiving honesty for the most part.

4. He can be delightfully witty when describing a positive and healthy relationship but also merciless in his condemnation; especially when it is destructive and exploitative, as it is more often than not.

5. After describing the harsh conditions in the village of Burgeo in the north of Newfoundland, he reveals the lure of the place; abundant fish, seals, dolphins, and whales.

Activity 45-7

45d Using semicolons effectively

Edit the following passage so that it includes only those semicolons that are effective.

Let there be no doubt that George Will is the quintessential conservative, and a widely read one at that; his message has a way of permeating the nation's political ear. He is perhaps the most widely syndicated columnist of the last decade; at least four hundred newspapers carry his column. His thoughts are expressed regularly in magazines, and his books have been reviewed by countless journals; however, no reviewer seems to agree with all of Will's ideas. Will seems to think that he knows what America needs to hear; America, for its part, seems to be listening.

Activity 45-8 (Editing 5 in Chapter 45 of *The Blair Handbook*)

45   Semicolons

Edit the following passage, using semicolons correctly. More than one edited version is possible.

What I like best about Spalding Gray's writing is that it is so personal. He tells the reader not only what happened, but also how he felt. Although some of the experiences he writes about are somewhat out of the ordinary, he always manages to find something everyone can relate to. Gray is not just a writer, though. He's also a monologist and an actor. He did not write down his first ten monologues, the first of which was an exercise in his acting class. Instead, he simply told them over and over. In fact, when Gray first started writing down his stories; he found it very difficult. He felt as if he had lost his personal voice and rhythm. He decided in the end to rework the transcripts of his monologues from his performances and put them into writing. Luckily, he was successful. He managed to preserve his unique and personal quality, and now, whether his story is told in person or on the page; it is absolutely riveting.

■ ■ ■
Colons

Edit the following passage, making sure that colons are used correctly to introduce examples, explanations, lists, and quotations and to separate certain elements.

After my last semester of college, four of my friends and I rented a house by the ocean for one week. We had one goal in mind to be together one last time before we would go to our separate ways. Our vacation turned out to be idyllic. During the day, we: went to the beach, read dime-store novels that we found in the basement, and worked on a 1,500-piece jigsaw puzzle, which had a biblical theme; the Last Supper. Around 7.00 we would have our dinner and then spend the evening: talking, watching a movie, or playing a game. We usually played one of three games: Scrabble, charades, or one that my friends and I invented, called: "Literary Quotations." The game is played as follows, one person suggests a subject, and each player tries to come up with a quotation from literature on that subject. For example: one night Emma proposed "sleep" as a theme, and Pamela promptly spoke these lines from Homer's *Odyssey*, "There is a time for words and there is also a time for sleeping." Bob added these words from Cervantes's *Don Quixote*, "Blessings light upon him that first invented this same sleep!" LeeAnn spoke up, "As Hamlet said: 'To sleep— perchance to dream: ay there's the rub.'" The game sounds difficult, but I surprised myself with how many times I was able to remember fitting quotes. I guess my four years as an English major were worth it after all!

Activity 46-2 (Editing 2 in Chapter 46 of *The Blair Handbook*)

46a Using colons as marks of introduction

46b Using colons as marks of separation

Edit the following sentences, using colons correctly.

1. One thing is certain, the new person on the job always has to do the worst chores.

2. Given the terrible weather of the last few days, I was relieved by what I saw out in the distance, a nice, calm ocean.

3. I stepped on the deck and spoke these words from Melville's Moby Dick. "Call me Ishmael."

4. The sight of my first whale made me think of Jonah 1.17-2.10.

5. Finally, I began the job I had been hired to do, preparing snacks and beverages in the galley.

6. We spotted various kinds of whales on the excursion, right whales, humpback whales, finback whales, and minke whales.

7. There is one thing whale watch enthusiasts should always remember to do, wear rubber-soled shoes.

8. The people on the deck wore clothes to keep them dry; ponchos and garbage bags.

9. When we returned at 600, I wanted nothing more than to go home and sleep.

10. One more chore awaited me however, scrubbing the slime off the sides of the boat.

Activity 46-3

46c Avoiding misuses of colons

Edit the following sentences, using a colon correctly in each one. Some sentences can be edited in more than one way. Circle the number of any sentence that is correct.

1. For many years before war actually broke out, Britain kept demanding: that the increasingly prosperous and independent colonies pay taxes to Britain.

2. The colonists rebelled, basing their resistance on the principle: that there should be no taxation without representation in the British Parliament.

3. Two major events that occurred in the Boston area were: the Boston Tea Party and the Boston Massacre.

4. Paul Revere, immortalized in a poem by Henry Wadsworth Longfellow, rode on horseback to Lexington: to issue a warning to the Minutemen that the British were coming.

5. Important battles of the Revolutionary War include the following Massachusetts battles: Lexington, Concord, and Bunker Hill.

■ Activity 46-4

Edit the following passage, using colons correctly and deleting colons that are used incorrectly. More than one edited version is possible.

Last summer, while I was painting a house adjacent to a retirement home, I got a chance to spend time with some of the residents. Ten to twenty older men would congregate in what they called "The Pub," a room at contained: tables comfortable chairs, a small bar, a pool table, and a television set. Each day at exactly 430 P.M. the social hour at the pub began for the staff and residents. I got to know a few of these men and learned to appreciate their special qualities, their personalities, their keen senses of humor; and their phenomenal memories. One resident liked to quote: the following lines from Yeats's "Sailing to Byzantium"—"An aged man is but a paltry thing. / A tattered coat upon a stick, unless / Soul clap its hand and sing, and louder sing / For every tatter in its mortal dress." At this point sometimes someone would applaud and say: "Encore!" These very special men had seen many days, that they still had much life in them. They seemed very wise to me: aged in the finest sense of the word.

■ ■ ■

Apostrophes

■ **Activity 47-1**

Edit the following passage, making sure that apostrophes are used correctly.

Imagine the flurry of excitement that must have rippled though the room at the mathematicians's meeting in Cambridge, England in the spring of 93. Until that day, no one had ever dreamt that Fermat's Last Theorem would one day be proved. No one except Princeton Universitys Andrew Wiles, that is, who's lifelong obsession had been to find the proof that had eluded Ph.D.s for more than 350 years. Finding it's proof had nagged at Wiles most of his' life, even as a child, when he first came across the theorem in a library book. Pierre de Fermat worked out his' famous theorem in 1637, jotting it down in the margin of a book. He did'nt have room, however, for the theorems proof of the books' margin. He had room only to explain, that, although he'd worked out a wonderful proof for his theorem, he did'nt have room to show it. For seven year's before he solved it, Wiles attention was directed almost exclusively toward proving the theorem, but almost no one knew what he was working on. Rumors circulated at the mathematicians's meeting when it became known that Wiles would speak on Fermat's last theorem. Little did the participants expect, however, that they're colleague had actually solved the most famous puzzle of modern mathematics.

Activity 47-2 (Editing I in Chapter 47 of *The Blair Handbook*)

47a Using apostrophes to form the possessive case of nouns and indefinite pronouns

Edit the following sentences, using apostrophes correctly to form the possessive of nouns and indefinite pronouns. Circle the number of any sentence that is correct.

1. The childrens spirits lifted when they saw the snow accumulating, since they knew it was their local school boards' tendency to close for inclement weather.

2. To many peoples' surprise, schools were open.

3. The storms' gale force winds howled for hours, and their strength caused a branch of my neighbors' oak tree to snap.

4. Stranded passenger's cars could be seen dotting the turnpike, abandoned in the storms' white-out conditions.

5. For most people, it will be several day's work to extricate their cars from the snow and ice.

6. The various cities' snow removal budgets were depleted even before the blizzard's first flakes fell.

7. The day before the storm hit, grocery store's long checkout lines attested to everyones expectations that they would be snowed in for a long time.

8. The storm's devastation could be seen from New England to Florida. Without a doubt it caused the eastern state's worst damage of the century.

■ **Activity 47-3**

47b Using apostrophes to form certain plurals

Edit the following sentences, using apostrophes where needed to form plurals, and eliminating unnecessary apostrophes. Circle the number of any sentence that is correct.

1. During the 1800's, in many places women were legally prohibited from getting a college education.

2. Few women earned B.A.s, let alone M.A.s or Ph.D.s.

3. Young girls were taught their ABC's at home, but they were not exposed to more than the rudiments of learning.

4. Early on, women entered male-dominated classes in two's and three's, but very quickly their numbers grew.

5. Any expectations that women would not be able to achieve As and Bs were easily dispelled as they proved to be just as intelligent and capable as men.

Activity 47-4 (Editing 2 in Chapter 47 of *The Blair Handbook*)

47c Using apostrophes to form contractions

Edit the following sentences, using apostrophes correctly to form contractions.

1. In the summer there's a boat that takes passengers from the city to Bear Mountain, where hiking enthusiasts wont be disappointed.

2. The views from the mountain's 1300-foot summit cant be surpassed; youll see wilderness stretching out before your eyes in every direction.

3. A trip to the country wouldnt be complete without a stop at Buddy's Café n Deli.

4. Hyde Park is home to FDR's country mansion, which has been preserved as it was when he died in 45.

5. You cant go wrong in the Hudson River Valley if what you like is stunning scenery, great hiking possibilities and rich history.

Activity 47-5 (Editing 3 in Chapter 47 of *The Blair Handbook*)

47d Avoiding misuses of the apostrophe

Edit the following sentences, being careful to distinguish plurals, contractions, and possessives.

1. Its perhaps surprising to learn that Dickens didn't start out as a novelist; instead, he trained as a lawyer's clerk.

2. The author, who's literary career began during the 1830's started out writing for magazines' under the pseudonym "Boz."

3. Society's evil, corruption, and crime were concerns to Dickens, and their frequently found as themes throughout his novels.

4. They're style and structure were affected by the fact that Dickens wrote his novel's for publication in monthly installments.

5. Dickens's first novel was *Pickwick Papers,* who's monthly installments were accompanied by plates created by a popular artist.

Activity 47-6 (Editing 5 in Chapter 47 of *The Blair Handbook*)

Edit the following passage, using apostrophes correctly.

In ancient Athens, after some of the Acropolis early buildings were destroyed by the Persians during the Persian War; the Athenian leader Pericles decided to rebuild many of the structures on the citys' chief fortress and sanctuary. The Parthenon was begun in 447 B.C. From anyones point of view, the columns of the temple appear to be straight, but in fact their built with a slight outward bulge. Its a subtle optical effect added for appearances sake. It works, too: one really cant tell that they arent straight. A huge amount of the Athenians's financial resources were used to rebuild the Parthenon, and to the Athenians it became a symbol of they're strength in the ancient world.

Quotation Marks

Edit the following passage, making sure that quotation marks are used correctly.

When I asked the director of the Center for Career Development what determines the kind of job a student gets after graduation, she replied, "Well, it depends on the type of student." "From my many years in this business, she said, I can say that students fall into different categories. She explained, "Some students are what I call "action students;" they jump right in and get involved with the center and keep using it until they find a really good job." Other students she defined as 'Micawbers,' (after the character in Dickens's *David Copperfield* who always expected things to turn out well for him without any effort on his part). These students think that their dream job will land in their lap, she said, and so they put off doing anything about finding it as long as possible As Donald Robert Perry Marquis so eloquently put it, 'Procrastination is the / art of keeping/ up with yesterday'." "To get them thinking about finding a job, we send out copies of articles they might find interesting, such as *Campus Life*'s *Tips on Landing a Great First Job*,' and we encourage them to come in and meet us. Most of the Micawbers do eventually involve themselves in finding a job, but only after putting it off as long as possible, and few of them find the ideal job." A third kind of student she called "wanderers"; these never seek career guidance, and they continue to wander even once they are out of school. "Which one are you, and are you happy with your attitude?," she inquired.

Activity 48-2 (Editing 2 in Chapter 48 of *The Blair Handbook*)

48a Using quotation marks for brief direct quotations

Edit the following sentences, using quotation marks correctly with brief direct quotations.

1. "Nobody even bothers to get dressed up to see the president, one senator said. That takes a little getting used to for those of us older senators."

2. "Even though Clinton holds the highest office in the country, he has never told us "You have to call me Mr. President now,"" said a former campaign organizer.

3. "The president keeps such long hours that the White House kitchen stays open until late at night," one adviser said. And the food is really good, too."

4. "If I had to choose one word to describe the atmosphere under the new administration, I'd have to say "unpredictable," a recent visitor said.

5. "An Elvis impersonator entertained here last week," a visitor added. Like my friend said, this White House is "a lot less uptight" than it ever was."

Activity 48-3 (Editing 4 in Chapter 48 of *The Blair Handbook*)

48d Using quotation marks for certain titles

Edit the following sentences, using quotation marks correctly with titles. Circle the number of any sentence that is correct.

1. Jan prefers to stay at home and finish reading *A View from the Woods*, one of the stories in Flannery O'Connor's *Everything That Rises Must Converge.*

2. As usual, Kim will be watching *Star Trek* reruns on television. Her favorite episode is *Who Mourns for Adonis?*

3. Erik will spend the evening reading "Why I Write," an essay that Orwell wrote the year after he published his novel *Animal Farm.*

4. Alan wants to stay home and study Thomas Hardy's poem *At the Word 'Farewell.'*

5. Jeff decides to stay at home and listen to his jazz records. He always turns up the volume when the song *Basin Street Blues* comes on.

150

Activity 48-4

48e Using quotation marks for translations, specialized terms, ironic usages, and some nicknames

Edit the following sentences, using quotation marks correctly with translations, specialized terms, ironic usages, and some nicknames.

1. Anyone can tell from their tofuburgers and sandals that Alice and Paul are the quintessential crunchy granolas.

2. They are easily persuaded by what is called green marketing, efforts by large corporations to convince consumers that their products are environmentally safe.

3. Their laid-back lifestyle probably comes from the fact that they live on the Left Coast, as California is sometimes called.

4. Since moving to California, their *joie de vivre*, or enjoyment of living, has increased greatly.

5. When they lived on the East Coast, Alice complained of feeling motivationally deficient, as the politically correct would say. In other words, she felt lazy.

Activity 48-5 (Editing 5 in Chapter 48 of *The Blair Handbook*)

48f Using other punctuation with quotation marks

Edit the following sentences, adding quotation marks as needed and making sure that other punctuation marks are used correctly.

1. What you don't understand Dr. Burton explained, is that with animal research, we can test hypotheses and isolate variables. She sighed. Let me tell you about—she started to say.

2. I don't deny that animal research can yield valuable information, he interrupted. My problem is about whether it is morally defensible.

3. "Morally defensible!" she exclaimed. We're talking about saving lives! Because animal research leads to medical breakthroughs that benefit human beings, she added, I would call it a necessary evil.

4. "Just because we humans have a superior intellect, Sam suggested, does not mean that we should exploit less intelligent animals."

5. She replied I think we should draw a distinction not between more intelligent and less intelligent animals, but between human and nonhuman animals.

6. There is a distinction, Sam agreed. Humans are the only animals with a conscience. Knowing that, we should listen to that conscience, he added.

Activity 48-6

48h Avoiding misuses of quotation marks

Edit the following sentences by deleting misused quotation marks. If you are uncomfortable using a term without quotation marks, use a substitute term. Some sentences can be edited in more than one way. Circle the number of any sentence that is correct.

1. About three feet down the slope he lost his balance. After that, it was all "downhill."

2. Lance "Hotdog" Davies raced over toward the expert's slope and went flying down the

    supergiant slalom course.

3. Arnold should think about taking up golf instead of skiing. Then he won't get so "teed"

    off.

4. He tried bowling once, but he said it wasn't really up his "alley."

5. I don't know if I will be successful in persuading Arnold to give up skiing for baseball,

    but I'll give it my best "pitch."

Activity 48-7 (Editing 6 in Chapter 48 of *The Blair Handbook*)

Edit the following passage to make sure that quotation marks and related punctuation are used correctly.

With the election in 1992 of Bill Clinton, the first baby boomer president, many people were excited by the possibility of change. One of the many baby boomers in the electorate said, "finally, I can really identify with the leader of my country." "I think he's going to effect some real changes." For the first time America had a president who grew up listening to the "The White Album," who read "Rolling Stone" magazine, who even named his daughter after *Chelsea Morning,* a popular song from the seventies. His running mate, Al Gore, also had concerns that they shared, especially an interest in environmental issues, which earned him the nickname Ozone Man in Republican circles. The Bush administration's attitude at the "Earth Summit," an international conference held in June 1992 to discuss environmental issues, had disappointed many voters. Already impatient for change on a number of other issues, voters looked to the Clinton-Gore team to be the voice of their environmental concerns as well.

Other Punctuation

■ **Activity 49-1**

Edit the following passage, using parentheses, dashes, brackets, and slashes. More than one edited version is possible.

Lying close to the Statue of Liberty in New York Bay is tiny Ellis Island tiny is size but certainly not in importance. A single building occupies the island. Originally that building was a fort—1808—later an arsenal, and finally it took shape as we know it, an immigration station. Over a sixty-year period 1891—1954, officials at Ellis Island welcomed or, in many cases, rejected immigrants who had come from Europe to America the "melting pot" of the world's nations. The number of immigrants who came is staggering, more than twenty million, and most Americans today are either descended from or know someone who is descended from an Ellis Island immigrant. (My great-grandmother came through Ellis Island from Poland on 08/08/08. Although she was a very young child (four years old), she can clearly remember the experience.) For the arriving boatloads of Europeans, America's attractions were many, including a: freedom from persecution and b: the possibility of living a prosperous life. For a fictionalized account of one immigrant's arrival in America, read Mark Helprin's Ellis Island [Dell Publishers, 1982].

Activity 49-2 (Editing I in Chapter 49 of *The Blair Handbook*)

49a Using parentheses

Edit the following sentences, inserting parentheses where appropriate and deleting parentheses that are unnecessary. You may need to make other changes in punctuation. Some sentences can be edited in more that one way.

1. In Europe, railroads were a major factor in the Industrial Revolution, see pp. 300–24.

2. England was the first country to open a public railroad, called "railway" by the British.

3. The first railroad to carry passengers began running in England in 1825–___?.

4. In some cases railroads grew on top of smaller tracks that were already in place in various industries, for example, in mining.

5. U.S. railroads were built to take advantage of the commerce and industry in the newly settled West, in those days Ohio was considered the West.

6. The rails were laid on wood, later concrete, cross ties (Modern railroads use continuous welded rails).

Activity 49-3

49b Using dashes

Edit the following passage, inserting dashes wherever they are required.

The transcendentalist movement taking its name from a belief that was important in life transcended human comprehension flourished in New England in the mid-1800s. Its followers sought to bring together all kinds of people. Rich or poor, man or woman, old or young it didn't matter in the least to its proponents. The inspiration for the movement came from German idealists Kant in particular as well as from Eastern mystical philosophies. Its influence was felt in American literature Melville and Hawthorne's works, for example, and politics.

Activity 49-4 (Editing 3 in Chapter 49 of *The Blair Handbook*)

49b Using dashes

Edit the following passage, deleting dashes where they are not effective. More than one edited version is possible.

Jamaica Kincaid's most openly opinionated—and, to my mind, best—book—*A Small Place*—is a social critique of her home island—Antigua. In this book, her voice—humble yet strong, and sometimes filled with anger—speaks for her people. Her feelings—stemming from years of living in Antigua in the aftermath of British imperialism—are expressed in simple—yet beautiful—manner.

Activity 49-5 (Editing 4 in Chapter 49 of *The Blair Handbook*)

49c Using ellipsis points

Using ellipsis points, edit the following paragraph to shorten it for a paper on racism. More than one edited version is possible.

"Until we label an out-group it does not clearly exist in our minds. Take the curiously vague situation that we often meet when a person wishes to locate responsibility on the shoulders of some out-group whose nature he cannot specify. In such a case he usually employs the pronoun 'they' without an antecedent. 'Why don't they make these sidewalks wider?' 'I hear they are going to build a factory in this town and hire a lot of foreigners.' 'I won't pay this tax bill; they can just whistle for their money.' If asked 'who?' the speaker is likely to grow confused and embarrassed. The common use of the orphaned pronoun *they* teaches us that people often want and need to designate out-groups (usually for the purpose of venting hostility) even when they have no clear conception of the out-group in question. And so long as the target of wrath remains vague and ill-defined specific prejudice cannot crystalize around it. To have enemies we need labels."

Activity 49-6 (Editing 5 in Chapter 49 of *The Blair Handbook*)

49d Using brackets

Edit the following passage, using brackets correctly.

According to the findings of a new study, people who smoke may be hurting not only themselves. "It (tobacco smoke) can be just as detrimental to nonsmokers as to smokers," a spokesperson for the study told reporters. "In fact, secondhand smoke may be even more dangerous," she added, "since they (nonsmokers) are inhaling it without a filter." This latest finding adds to the growing list of the dangers of cigarette smoking. (See the related article on the effects of smoking on fetal development (p. 14).)

■ Activity 49-7

49c Using ellipsis points

49d Using brackets

The following passage is from an essay on Elvis Presley. Using ellipsis points and brackets as necessary, edit the passage as if you were going to quote from it in a formal research paper on popular culture in the American South. More than one edited version is possible.

Elvis was the most popular entertainer in the world, but nowhere as popular as in his native South. In the last years of his career, his audience in other parts of the country was generally centered in the original "fifties" fans whose youth and music were defined by Elvis, and in the lower or working class people who saw in Elvis some glamorized image of their own values. In the South, however, the pattern of Elvis's popularity tended to cut across age barriers and class lines which were themselves a less recognizable thing in a region which almost no one is more than a generation or two away from poverty, and where "class" in small communities might have more to do with family and past status than with money. Among Southern youth, Elvis was not a relic from a musical past; he was still one of the vital forces behind a Southern rock, which though different now from his, still echoes the rhythms which his music had fused out of the region.

Linda Ray Pratt, "Elvis, or the Ironies of Southern Identity"

■ Activity 49-8 (Editing 7 in Chapter 49 of *The Blair Handbook*)

Edit the following paragraph, using parentheses, dashes, and brackets correctly. More than one edited version is possible.

When you're in the business of selling something, whether it be books or balloons you find out pretty quickly that the market isn't stationery (sic). That means you have to keep moving too. But how do you find new markets for your product? You should know from the outset that learning about them isn't easy for many reasons, such as the following: a: you might not have personal contacts for example, acquaintances to give you leads, b: you might not have much money for research, c: you might not be very knowledgeable about a certain area, and d: there might not be much information about them (new markets) when you start selling your product. There are thank goodness! a few things you can do to offset the difficulties, though. Keep up with the professional journals and handbooks there's a new one available every month, it seems. And remember to keep smiling, your biggest sale ever could be right around the corner!

Spelling

Edit the following passage, making sure there are no misspelled words.

Most college instructors have a very prejudice view of human intelligence. They basicly define intelligence as the ability to solve complex mathmatical problems or to conduct origanal research in labratories or to express complicated ideas in writting. Students can "prove" there intelligence only by getting high marks in as many subjects as possable. However, knowledgable psychologists have begun to view human intelligence alot more broadly then before, and they now believe that many diffrent kinds of intelligence may be studied and measurred all by themselfs with new tests and methods. According to this arguement, for example, artistic ability is a special kind of intelligence, present from berth, that allows a person to percieve reality in a way that other people can not and then to translate those perceptions into unique phyzical forms. Excellence at foot ball and other sports requirs another kind of intelligence that many researchers guess is largly unconscience but that still involves speciallized mental abilities present even in babys. If even athaletes could be reconized for there inborn intelligence, the affect on education would be truely revolutionary.

Activity 50-2 (Editing I in Chapter 50 of *The Blair Handbook*)

50a Checking for commonly confused words

Edit the following passage, looking for commonly confused words.

"Were just about to have our desert. Would you care to join us?"

"Thanks allot, but no. I've all ready eaten—a four-coarse meal."

"Oh, just have one small peace of pie. You can have it plane, without any topping."

"It looks extrodinary, but to tell you the truth, I'm a little afraid of the affect it'll have on my waste. I've been trying to loose weight; my cloths are getting so tight I can hardly breath."

"Are you getting any exorcise? That's probly the best way to lose weight."

"We'll, I never was much of an athalete, as you know. I have a stationery bike, but I just can not seem to motivate myself to workout. I always seem to find an excuse to put it off until latter."

"I no just what you mean. It's really difficult. And than when I don't exorcise, I have such a guilty conscious."

"Heres an idea: Why don't we lesson or guilt and meat tomorrow morning at the tennis courts?"

"Alright! Your on!"

Activity 50-3 (Editing 2 in Chapter 50 of *The Blair Handbook*)

50b Using basic spelling rules

Edit the following passage, using basic spelling rules to eliminate misspelled words.

Early in my senior year of high school, I had to make the very tough decision about where I wanted to go to college. I sent away for brochures and catalogs from a number of schools, and when I received them, I leaved threw them to get some ideas of colleges that offered programs in the engineering feild. I was hoping to get into one of the colleges or universitys in the Midwest, specificly in the state of Michigan. I looked into attendding the University of Michigan, and I saw that it had quite an extensive engineering program. I have an aunt who majorred in mechanical engineering at the University of Michigan, so she is very knowledgable about the program. She told me that it is basicly a very good program, but that it is also a lot of work. The curriculum offers many different courses leading to a bachelor of science degree. Some of the major subjects are design, solid and fluid mechanics, manufactureing processes and systems, and thermodynamics. In addition to these courses, six courses in the humanitys and social sceince feilds are required. After considerring it for a week, I decided that the University of Michigan was where I would go to get my college education.

■ ■ ■
Capitalization

■ Activity 51-1

Edit the following passage for problems with capitalization.

My family lived in Yeehaw for two years (It seemed more like a century), and while we were there my Sister Joy and I attended Franklin senior high school. The building was a run-down three-story structure that looked like it had barely survived World war II. It was about a mile South of our house on Joel street, and although we could have taken the bus, on our first day of school Joy said, "let's avoid contact for as long as possible," so we got into the habit of walking.

From early Fall through christmas of that year, we tried to make the best of what we both agreed was a bad situation. The principal was fat and bald, wore Cowboy boots and a string tie, and called the boys "Pardners" and the girls "Little ladies." Our English teacher was like a dr. seuss character; she was tall with a long thin neck and hair that stood straight up on her head, and she introduced herself the first day of class by saying, "My name is mrs. Hamm. Mrs. Hamm I am." We spent the first six weeks reading *Romeo And Juliet*, which according to her had two main shakespearean themes: (1) young people living during the renaissance talked a lot better than young people today. (2) It never pays to listen to a catholic priest.

Activity 51-2

51a Capitalizing the first word of a sentence

Edit the following passage, using a capital letter at the beginning of every sentence or deliberate sentence fragment. More than one edited version is possible.

Why do some people become addicts while others do not? Does it have to do with genetics? personality types? environmental factors? Some behavioral scientists believe that alcoholics are particular personality types. Long-term studies indicate that specific personality traits show up early in life: Children who are impulsive and easily distracted might, for instance, turn into addicts later in life. (of course, some impulsive, easily distracted children do not become addicts.) Not all scientists ascribe to the personality-type theory, however. Another group believes that the answer lies in the following area: The study of genetic indicators. These scientists engage in studies on identical twins, hoping to shed light on who is at risk of becoming an addict.

Activity 51-3

51b Capitalizing quotations and lines of poetry

Edit the following passage to make capitalization in quotations correct.

"It feels really cold," Susan said, bending down to dip her hand into the water. "And it's only September."

"Poor Champ!" Dan replied. "he must be freezing."

"Who?" Susan asked. "who's Champ? What are you talking about?"

"Don't tell me you've never heard of Champ!" Dan said in disbelief. "He's Lake Champlain's answer to the Loch Ness monster."

"Are you pulling my leg," Susan inquired, "Or is this for real?"

"It's real," Dan said. "I swear! You've never heard any of the stories about a sea serpent living in this lake? Dozens of people have reported seeing him. Samuel de Champlain wrote about him first," he explained. "in his log, he described a giant sea serpent with bubble eyes, horns on his head, and a round barrel body."

"So now I'm supposed to believe that not only is there a mysterious creature in the lake," Susan said skeptically, "But that this creature has been alive for nearly four hundred years! How gullible to you think I am?"

"It's not the same creature," Dan replied. "obviously there has been more than one Champ. I can see that you still don't believe me. Let's go over to the library and you can read the articles for yourself."

"All right," Susan replied, "But you'll never convince me that he is real."

Activity 51-4

51c Capitalizing proper nouns and their derivatives

Edit the following sentences, correcting the capitalization of nouns and their derivatives.

1. Nixon's opponent in the november election was senator George McGovern from south Dakota.

2. Attorney general John Mitchell ran Nixon's campaign.

3. One year before the 1972 election, the twenty-sixth amendment had given eighteen-year-olds the right to vote.

4. The scandal that led to president Nixon's downfall is known as watergate. It is named after the office building where the democratic national committee had its Headquarters.

5. The President abused his Presidential powers by using Government Agencies, such as the federal bureau of investigation and the CIA, to spy on people.

6. In the midst of the Watergate investigations during the Fall of 1973, war broke out in the middle east on yom kippur.

7. Investigators proved that the republican abuses involved many Agencies, including the cia, fbi, and the irs.

8. During the televised senate investigation, millions of americans—from the big apple to L.A.—were glued to their television sets.

9. The investigation gripped the viewers' attention, much like the iran-contra hearings or the confirmation of supreme court justice Clarence Thomas

10. Members of the U.S. congress was prepared to impeach Nixon, but he resigned before they could do so.

■ Activity 51-5

51d Capitalizing titles of books and other works

Edit the following sentences correctly capitalizing all titles.

1. Jack borrowed a book on one of our presidents—*RN: the Memoirs of Richard Nixon.*

2. The library has a fine collection of Tennessee Williams plays, including *The Night of the Iguana, Cat on a Hot Tin Roof,* and *a Streetcar Named Desire.*

3. The library's collection of books on the media is growing quickly. New additions are *Media Events: the Live Broadcasting of History* and *Behind the Front Page: a Candid History of how the News is Made.*

4. Patrons can borrow movies also. Mario chose *out of Africa* and *A Room With a View.*

5. Short story collections are shelved in the fiction section. Connie is looking for Jane Smiley's collection *The Age of Grief.* She wants to reread the stories "The Pleasure of her Company" and "Jeffrey, believe me."

Activity 51-6 (Editing 1 in Chapter 51 of *The Blair Handbook*)

Edit the following passage, using capital letters according to the guidelines in this chapter.

The renaissance, a term that means "rebirth," began in italy in the mid-fourteenth century and spread throughout western Europe by the middle of the sixteenth century. and what a time of rebirth! With the help of numerous patrons of the arts, such as the Medici Family in Florence, learning, literature, and the arts flourished. Lorenzo de' Medici was the influential patron of the great artist Botticelli, whose works include *The birth of Venus* and *La primavera.* (the works of Botticelli became great favorites of the Pre-Raphaelites.)

The pursuit of literature and the arts was also fostered by Popes, such as Pope Nicholas V. Petrarch and Boccaccio were among the first writers to become interested in secular literature. Before the renaissance, most of the literature read in their christian society had been related to the church. During the Renaissance, an interest in reading latin and greek literature grew, and many people put their energy into collecting manuscripts, often ransacking monastic libraries throughout europe to obtain them. Countless old manuscripts are now housed in many of the great museums and libraries of the world, including the British museum.

The Renaissance was also a turning point in philosophy and science. Galileo and Copernicus, for example, made great discoveries in the field of astronomy.

Hyphenation

■ **Activity 52-1**

Edit the following passage making sure that all words are hyphenated correctly.

Since the mid 1970s, government expenditures for welfare have mush-roomed, with nearly a two thirds increase in outlays from 1985-present. While some of these out of control costs are the result of bureaucratic mis-management and client fraud, the essential problem is that more and more people are applying for welfare and staying on welfare rolls longer. This is due in-part to a down-turn in the economy in the postReagan years; but it must also be admitted that welfare policies over the last twenty five years have created a "culture of poverty," a self defeating cycle that discourages any attempt on the part of recipients to work and to save. Pro and anti welfare forces dis-agree on many issues, but they have come to-gether on one matter: welfare recipients must be given opportunites to get them-selves off welfare. Thus, any attempt at welfare-reform must be part of an allinclusive package the includes education and re-training, child care, health care, and carefully-developed programs encouraging personal-and-family responsibility. Reformminded individuals must accept the fact that there is no easy cureall for the welfare problem.

Activity 52-2 (Editing I in Chapter 52 of *The Blair Handbook*)

52a Hyphenating words at the ends of lines

Indicate the best place for hyphenating each of the following words. Not all words should be hyphenated. You may want to use a dictionary to check your hyphenation.

1. coordinated

2. acquitted

3. preparedness

4. width

5. crossbones

6. minibus

7. ignite

8. overcast

9. commitment

10. antidote

■ Activity 52-3

52a Hyphenating words at the ends of lines

Indicate the best place for hyphenating each of the following words. If a word contains more than two syllables, indicate all possible hyphenation points. Not all words should be hyphenated. You may want to use a dictionary to check your hyphenation.

1. wrecked

2. macroeconomics

3. enough

4. preamble

5. counterbalance

6. recessed

7. eavesdrop

8. discernment

9. reunification

10. against

■ Activity 52-4

52b Hyphenating after some prefixes
52c Hyphenating to link parts of compound words

Edit the following sentences, using hyphens when necessary and deleting unnecessary hyphens.

1. The new mayor is a selfassured woman whose attitude is strongly pro business.

2. The above mentioned former mayor re-ceived very few votes from pre or post-retirement voters.

3. Many people criticized him for supposedly unAmerican ideas and for his lack of support for the Canada U.S. trade agreement.

4. The new mayor hopes to recreate jobs in the inner city.

5. She plans to re-vive industry and bring pro-ductivity to pre-existing levels.

6. Skeptics doubt that her plan will lead to the re-covery she has promised.

7. Her team of socalled experts is not well-regarded by the former mayor's advisers.

8. She expects to restore the city to pre 1980 levels of prosperity.

9. If the economy re-covers, more people will be self sufficient.

10. At his farewell address, the exmayor ex-pressed his desire to reenter politics someday.

Activity 52-5

52d Hyphenating in fractions, numbers, and units of measure

Edit the following sentences to make sure that all fractions, numbers, and units of measure are hyphenated correctly.

1. Each team member runs for 150-200 miles in a season.

2. Two thirds of the team also competed last year.

3. The youngest runner, a seventeen year-old, thinks she can beat last year's champion,

   who is nineteen years old.

4. The coach insists on a ninety minute practice every day.

5. The team's best time is in the 60 yard dash.

Activity 52-6 (Editing 2 in Chapter 52 of *The Blair Handbook*)

Edit the following passage, hyphenating all words where necessary and deleting unnecessary hyphens. You may have to consult a dictionary.

Twenty five years ago, Massachusetts was in a state of steady decline. The economy of the pre 1970s had been built upon industries that were now out of date and rundown. Unemployment was on the rise, and the future looked grim for the state's residents. But early in the 1970s, the situation began to improve, as Massachusetts embarked on what became known as the "Massachusetts Miracle." Thanks to an ex-plosion of high tech industries and products such as mini-computers, the economy started to turn around dramatically. Pre-existing industries began to die out, and the economy boomed with new industries, new companies, and new jobs for thousands of previously-unemployed workers. With more hightech companies than any-where in the country except California's well known Silicon Valley, Massachusetts became one of the wealthiest states. Its prosperity seemed neverending. Literally thousands of companies were started in Massachusetts from 1973–1988. But prosperity did not last. By the late 1980s, with increasing world-wide competition and a flood of mini-computers on the market. Massachusetts began to feel the effects of the re-cession that struck the whole country. Even to-day, the state's residents struggle to re-cover from the so called miracle.

■ ■ ■

Italics

■ **Activity 53-1**

Edit the following passage to make sure that words are italicized according to the guidelines of this chapter.

The Sex Life of Flowers, a book by Bastiaan Meeuse and Sean Morris, originated as an episode broadcast on public television's "Nature" series under the title *Sexual Encounters of the Floral Kind.* Like the documentary, the book is a fascinating look at the many unusual adaptations plants have made in order to achieve pollination. In Chapter 2, *The Flower,* the authors report that pollination among flowering plants (known by the biological term angiosperms) is generally an act of quid pro quo; that is, in order out *get* something (the pollen-carrying services of bees and other insects), flowers must *give* something in return (usually food, in the form of nectar). Consequently, flowers have developed shapes and colors designed to attract visitors to a *rendezvous* with the nectar inside. For example in the forget-me-not flower (Myosotis palustris), a bright yellow ring surrounds and highlights the dark entrance; the meadow cranesbill (Geranium pratense) offers a similar contrast by reflecting no ultraviolet light from the flower center. Like the male and female of other species, flowers and insects must be simpatico if the process of reproduction is to take place.

Activity 53-2

53a Italicizing titles

Edit the following sentences, using italics (and quotation marks) according to the guidelines in this chapter.

1. The book-length poems "Beowulf" and "The Divine Comedy" are often studied in freshman surveys of great books in Western literature.

2. *Afro-American Fragment* is the opening poem in a volume called *Selected Poems of Langston Hughes.*

3. "Mother Jones" and "The Nation" are both popular magazines that feature articles on public, social, and political affairs. Articles from such magazines are often excerpted and reprinted in the *Utne Reader.*

4. During the 1980s, syndicated columnist Anna Quindlen wrote a regular column in the "New York Times" called "Life in the Thirties." In 1988, her columns were collected and published in a book entitled "Living Out Loud."

5. The television program *National Geographic* featured coyotes, rattlesnakes, and mustangs on an episode called *The Animals Nobody Loved.*

Activity 53-3

53b Italicizing the names of individual trains, ships, airplanes, and spacecraft

53c Italicizing foreign words

Edit the following sentences, using italics as necessary. Delete any unnecessary italics. You may need to check a dictionary for some terms. Circle the number of any sentence that is correct.

1. Along the way she passed many different kinds of trees, including Quercus alba, Acer rubrum, and Abies balsamea.

2. The "Adirondack," Amtrak's day train to Montreal, is fine, but the night train is the *crème de la crème.*

3. While in Montreal, Louise visited museums and galleries and admired many wonderful *objets d'art.*

4. In a little French *café* in the old part of the city, Louise ordered *pâté, hors d'oeuvres,* and *vin de Bordeaux rouge.* She tried not to make a *faux pas* when ordering.

5. One day she went on a boat tour up the St. Lawrence River on the "Pride of Montreal." Unfortunately, because of the choppy waters, she suffered from *mal de mer.*

6. Louise is a bit of a bon vivant: She adores le boire et le manger in Montreal.

7. When it was time to leave, Louise sighed and said, "Tempus fugit—especially when you're having fun."

Activity 53-4

53d Italicizing for emphasis

53e Italicizing words, letters, and numbers used as words

Edit the following sentences, making sure that italics are used correctly for words presented as words and for emphasis. Circle the number of any sentence that is correct.

1. *Expressionism* is characterized by a *revolt* against realism.

2. In expressionist literature, authors represent the world not *objectively,* but rather *subjectively*—as it appears to them.

3. Expressionist painters often used *intense* colors and simple forms to convey strong emotions.

4. Surrealism is the name given to a movement that began in France around the same time as expressionism began in Germany.

5. *Surrealists* owed much to work of Freud; they emphasized dreams, fantasy, and the power of the *unconscious* over the *conscious* mind.

6. The term literature of the absurd is given to works founded on the belief that the human condition is essentially absurd.

7. *Literature of the absurd* has its roots in the movements of *expressionism* and *surrealism.*

Activity 53-5 (Editing I in Chapter 53 of *The Blair Handbook*)

Edit the following passage, making sure words are italicized appropriately.

Before planting a garden it is a good idea to consult a reputable source for tips on successful gardening. Many newspapers, such as the New York Times, have a weekly column devoted to gardening. There are also many useful books, such as "A Guide to Growing Gorgeous Greenery," with its especially useful introductory chapter, *Plan before You Plant.*

First a gardener should learn about the different types of plants. Annuals is the term given to plants that complete their lifetime in one year; the term *perennials* is used for plants that grow back every year: Many annuals are popular with gardeners, especially the Begonia semperflorens and the Petunia hybrida.

Another issue for gardeners to consider is pesticides. Environmentally conscious gardeners are not opposed to pesticides *per se*, but they use only organic pesticides, which derive from *natural* rather than *synthetic* substances. Gardening books are useful sans doute, and they may prevent the worst *faux pas* in the garden, but in the end there is no one way to make a garden—chacun à son goût!

■ ■ ■

Numbers

■ **Activity 54-1**

Edit the following passage to make sure that all numbers are handled appropriately.

It is hard to believe, but our present-day popcorn has roots going back at least five thousand six hundred years in the American Southwest and over 75 thousand years in Central and South America. A staple food in many early cultures, popcorn is now the most popular prepared snack food in the United States: it is estimated that as many as 2, 000, 000 bags are sold daily in movie theatres alone, representing just 1/8 of the total amount eaten.

Having smelled the aroma of popping corn wafting from local dorm rooms as early as 7 o'clock in the morning (and as late as four-thirty A.M.), my roommate and I decided to conduct an informal poll to see how popular popcorn is on campus. 70 students participated in our survey, which we conducted in front of the library for 2 1/2 hours a day over five days (the week of March thirteenth, 1992). Of the respondents, forty-eight percent were women and fifty-two percent were men, and the average age was twenty-two. Our questionnaire consisted of 12 questions (see Appendix A).

■ Activity 54-2 (Editing I in Chapter 54 of *The Blair Handbook*)

Edit the following passage, making sure all numbers are handled appropriately for non-technical writing.

At 10 o'clock this morning, after a seven-hour journey, the peacekeeping force turned back when stopped by a crowd of 300 demonstrators. At least 1/4 of the angry demonstrators were armed, and they claimed to have more than three thousand rounds of ammunition. The 33 trucks left the area and drove toward the nearest town sixty miles to the west. The peacekeeping force had been carrying food and medicine for the more than thirteen thousand five hundred sick and wounded citizens. That number will probably grow, with temperatures expected to drop below twenty degrees later this month.

■ Activity 54-3

Edit the following sentences, writing out numbers or using figures according to convention for nontechnical writing. Circle the number of any sentence that is correct.

1. In 2/3 of the states, math scores rose dramatically.

2. Increases in scores for verbal aptitude ranged from 2.6% to twenty-eight percent.

3. In one high school in the Northwest, ten students scored higher than 750 on the math test, 125 scored between 550 and 750, and 40 scored below 550.

4. The average age of the students who participated was sixteen.

5. The first part of the test began at nine A.M. and ended at 9:45.

6. Ninety-five percent of the schools reported their scores on time.

7. Statisticians pored over the 40,000 tests, analyzing data for 13 days.

8. An analysis of the results of the survey can be found on page twelve of today's newspaper.

9. The testing took place on October twelfth, 1992, and February eighteenth, 1993.

Abbreviations

Edit the following passage to make sure that abbreviations have been used according to the guidelines in this chapter.

Doctor Wm. Jensen, M.D., a prof. of medicine at Tulane University in New Orleans, had been missing for eight days when he was finally discovered wandering dazedly along Perry St. in downtown St. Petersburg, FL, at 9:15 pm on Sat., Feb. 13, 1993. He was wearing the same suit he was last seen in and had only 73¢ in his pocket. How the dr. got to St. Pete is a mystery yet to be solved; he remembers nothing about those missing eight days. His last memory is of driving from a meeting of the N.O. chapter of the AMA and stopping to help two motorists, apparently in distress. He believes he must have been hit on the head from behind as he stepped from his car. Family members, friends, etc. think it is likely that Jensen was drugged.

▪ Activity 55-2

Edit the following passage, using abbreviations as appropriate.

Although the United States Constitution is supposed to guarantee equal rights to all people regardless of color, in the first half of this century most African Americans in the southern U.S. lived in deplorable conditions. E.g., African Americans had to use separate washrooms, and they could not attend school with whites. Not until the 1940s did the United States Supreme Court finally begin to outlaw practices that deprived African Americans of their rights. One small step toward equality was made when representatives from the National Association for the Advancement of Colored People (N.A.A.C.P.) persuaded the Court that maintaining separate schools for African Americans and whites was not equal. In 1954, under Chief Justice Earl Warren of Calif., the Court ordered the desegregation of schools in the U.S. Despite the new legislation, however, the southern states still resisted integration, and only Senator Lyndon Johnson from TX and two sen. from Tenn. (Estes Kefauver and Albert Gore, Senior) were in favor of desegregating the schools. Racial conflict raged throughout the southern states over the issue of integration; one area of conflict was Little Rock, Ark., where resistance was so great that the National Guard had to be used to enforce integration. Even this drastic step did not solve the problem, however, and the struggle for equal education and other civil rights for African Americans went on for many years.

■ Activity 55–3

Edit the following sentences, making sure that abbreviations are used correctly. Circle the number of any sentence that is correct.

1. Prof. Smithers started the co-op because he was frustrated by the devastating effects of the recession.

2. Neighborhood residents line up outside the co-op around 6:00 a.m.

3. Whether it is 95° Fahrenheit or -15° Fahrenheit, there is always a long line of hungry people.

4. Next Sat., the mayor will visit the co-op. Mayor Ruth Brown has been a supporter of the co-op from the beginning.

5. The number of households receiving food stamps has increased 25 percent in the past two years.

6. Since unemployment has risen 3% in the past year, it is not surprising that the number of people requiring assistance has also risen.

7. When the co-op first opened, Senator Lillian Good held a news conference to increase public awareness of poverty.

8. With an annual budget of 60,000 dollars, the co-op is the main source of food for the community's low-income residents.

9. Each household receives two gal. of milk every week.

10. As part of his fundraising efforts, Dr. Smithers, Ph.D., has requested donations from local businesses.

11. Donations to the co-op may be sent to 34 N. Branch St., Willowdale, Ohio 44667.

■ ■ ■
Preparing the Final Manuscript

■ Activity 56-1

Proofread the following passage, correcting all errors in spelling, grammar, punctuation, and mechanics.

Originally panned by critic as noting more then a cheap shocker, Alfred Hitchcocks film

"Psycho" is now considered a cult classic and one of the directors greatest acheivements.

What most people remember best about the movie is the famous shower scene, in which

Janet Leigh is attacked by knive-wielding old lady. (Some flim historians have argue that

this scene was not acutally directed by Hitchcock but by Saul Bass his assistant director.

However, their are many other effective moments: The long introduction showing Janet

Leigh stealing money from the bank were she works and driving thorough the night to the

Bates motel, the detective, played by Martin Balsam, climbing the stair case in the old

house as he looks for Mrs. Bates, and, of course the climatic scene in the basement when

Vera Miles come face to face with with the skeleton of Mrs Bates. Alos adding alot to the

suspense of the movie is the sharp, black and white photography by John L. Russell, the

intnese music by Bernard Herrmann, and the truely eerie performance by Anthony Perkins'

in the central role of Norman/Mrs. Bates. A critic is entitled to their opinion, but most of

them were wrong about "Psycho" in 1960.

Activity 56-2 (Editing 2 in Chapter 56 of *The Blair Handbook*)

Proofread the following passage, correcting all errors in spelling, grammar, punctuation, and mechanics. Use standard proofreading marks.

Marian Anderson, who died in 1993, was the first black opera singer to preform at the

Metropoliton Opera (1955), and she became an inspiracion to generations of black

performers thoughout the U.S. Yet she was not able to make a name for herself in her own

county until late in her life because of raical discrimmination. Althrough her grate talent

was recognised early in her life (she won a voice contest in New York in 1925,) she could not

get any rolls in opera, and her carrer was going nowhere. In the 1930s, Anderson decided to

go to Europe to perform, and she quicky became an international singing star. When she

returned to the U.S. and was invited to sing in Washington, DC, the D.A.R. (Daughters of

the American Revolution) denied her acess to Constitution Hall, it's national headquarters.

Eleanor Roosvelt (along with several other women) resined from the D.A.R. over this

disgracefull incident, and she aranged for Anderson to perform outside at the Lincoln

Memorial. 75,000 people came to hear Anderson sing, and her performence in front of

Lincolns statute became a powerful cymbal of the civil right's movement.

Activity 56-3

Proofread the following passage, correcting all errors in spelling, grammar, punctuation, and mechanics. Use standard proofreading marks.

Erma Bombeck, columist and author of 9 books and countless articels, use wit and

sarcasm in telling her tales of housewife reppresion and thankless child rearing. Her own

experence in the feilds of motherhood and mariage are the largest facter contributeing to the

credability of her stories. Writen primarily between 1970-1979, Bobeck's works are

humourous attempts at understanding the most-pressing problems of the seventies, the two

predominent ones delt with her writing are the underated house-wife and the increasing

number fo teenaggers. Her books are all writen in a similer stile: they are colections of

stories based on her personel experienses and are filled with humor, vivacety, and

cleverness. Having viewed Bombeck's televized comentaries and read her books and articles,

she is obviously able to find humor in everything she encounters. That humor is often

convayed threw sarcasm, and she can be down-right negative and pesimmistic, yet

Bombeck is always abel to maintain a light-hearted and very funny style.